A tour de force in the call to a new unity. ⌐
with this quest and Malcolm has met thi.

Lyndon Bowring, ⌐⌐⌐⌐⌐⌐⌐ ⌐⌐⌐⌐⌐⌐⌐ ⌐⌐ ⌐⌐⌐⌐

A wonderful and insightful look at the clear biblical mandate for unity. I found myself captivated by the wisdom pouring from each page. Get it today and be inspired to play your part.

Gavin Calver, Director of Mission, Evangelical Alliance; Chair of Spring Harvest Planning Group

One For All *is not for the fainthearted. Malcolm Duncan calls us from our comfortable corners of opinion and denominationalism to engage in what the Bible actually says about the unity of the body of Christ. With a passionate heart, he challenges us to bravely and honestly examine the causes of disunity within the Church, and to set the "Bible as our plumbline against which we measure ourselves". This book is easy on the eyes, at times uncomfortable for the soul, but ultimately directs our purpose for unity as expressed by Jesus in John 17, "that the world might believe that You sent Me." Surely that's the resolve we all should strive for!*

Catherine Campbell, Author of *Chasing the Dawn* and *Broken Works Best*

One for All *calls the church to a Christian unity based not in fad or fashion but rooted in the foundation of Scripture. What makes it even more compelling is Malcolm Duncan's evident passion for the church, the real "flesh and blood", "warts and all" church to become what Christ has already purposed and prayed for it to be. This is a significant and timely book.*

Chris Cartwright, General Superintendent, Elim Pentecostal Churches

This book is both timely and helpful. With disarming honesty and genuine humility Malcolm digs into important Bible passages on the blessings of unity. Thank you Malcolm for this courageous message. Not everyone will agree with what you say but all can learn.

Bishop Ken Clarke

One for All *has captured what is for me a central theme of scripture and a key prophetic challenge that God wants to bring to the Church at this time: in the midst of amazing diversity as God's people, God has called us to recognise and celebrate our unity – being members of the same family, brothers and sisters in Christ. This is a unity which brings smiles in heaven and greater effectiveness on earth.*

Steve Clifford, General Director, Evangelical Alliance

When then church fails to address the issue of its own unity, then the world suffers. Study the biblical foundations and get ready for volume two on the implications!

David Coffey OBE, Global Ambassador BMS World Mission, Past President of the Baptist World Alliance

This is a book for our time! We live in a time when divisions within evangelicalism seem to increase rather than decrease. Malcolm calls us to take a long hard look at ourselves in the light of biblical teaching. He is honest about the challenges and even his own failures in maintaining unity. He urges us to consider that biblical unity "will not sacrifice truth on the altar of grace but nor will it sacrifice grace on the altar of truth". There is much in this book to challenge us. There is also encouragement to recognise and live out what it really means to be family.

Elaine Duncan, Chief Executive, Scottish Bible Society

Erudite and theologically robust. Malcolm Duncan engages with the issue of Christian unity with courage and clarity: courage, because the road he invites us to travel is devoid of sentimentality; clarity, because it is rooted in a rich pastoral ministry.

John Glass, Chair of Council, Evangelical Alliance; Former Elim General Superintendent

As a non conformist addressing a predominantly evangelical constituency, Malcolm winsomely challenges the default position of so many churches of all traditions where disunity and separation seem to be accepted as inevitable and unavoidable. His analysis is measured and compassionate but hard-hitting as he builds up a biblical case against the "blind spot" in which churches choose to tolerate disunity while yet professing to be thoroughly biblical. His concern is not about structural unity nor about lowest common denominator unity-at-all-costs. He is, however, passionate about a thoroughly biblical concern for truth matched by a deep resolve to love and engage with those Christians with whom we may differ, to the point where walking away from them is an absolute last resort. In the 500th anniversary year of Martin Luther's 95 theses, this is a timely and even prophetic book which flows from a strongly missional heart.

Rt Rev Ken Good, Bishop of Derry and Raphoe

The call to unity runs all the way through the New Testament: Jesus called us to it, Paul called us to do it, and yet still we struggle with it. In fact it is so hard that it is tempting to give up on unity entirely. This brilliant book reminds us of why unity is so important and why it is vital for the health and wellbeing of the church. It is a must-read for anyone serious about their faith and what it calls them to be and do.

Paula Gooder, Theologian in Residence, The Bible Society

Jesus didn't give us any language to explain how we would differ from each other within his Church. We use labels to explain our inevitable differences, but he gave us one common identity – "disciples". And he made clear that the mark of being his disciples would be unity expressing itself in love. Malcolm's wonderful book serves the body of Christ in a time of tensions and divisions by reminding us that we are, and could only ever be, one body.

Paul Harcourt, National Leader of New Wine England

The unity of the church is central to Christ's prayers for his people but is sadly so often missing from our priorities. In this timely book Malcolm Duncan shows us not just why unity matters to God but also how it can become a reality for us. He refuses to give pat answers or to back away from the real issues we face. You may not agree with all of his conclusions but you will be challenged by the grace of his approach and the courage of his convictions.

Dr Krish Kandiah, Founding director of Home for Good and author of God is Stranger

In this year, when we will be remembering the 500th anniversary of the beginning of the Reformation, One For All is a call to the church to commit again to unity. Not always the easy or simple route, but the route that pleases the heart of God and provides a strong foundation for the church's witness.

Billy Kennedy, Leader, Pioneer

It is almost scandalous that we have so little concern for the unity of God's people – here is an urgent and passionate book that offers help and hope. Malcolm Duncan offers profound encouragement from key Bible passages, grapples honestly with the contemporary challenges of church life, and demonstrates personal commitment to the cause of unity across *the country. A welcome and timely call to action for every church that is committed to the cause of Christ.*

Jonathan Lamb, Minister-at-large, Keswick Ministries, and Vice President of IFES

Like a warm and wise friend, Malcolm skilfully weaves together theology, church history and his own experiences, drawing us again and again to wrestle with the unity, rather than uniformity, that rests at the heart of God. One For All is an extraordinary book, a useful manual, a personal challenge and an absolute must-read for us all as we share faith, hope and love in a fractured world.

Cathy Madavan, writer, speaker, member of Spring Harvest planning group and author of *Digging for Diamonds*

National church leader and prophet Malcolm Duncan offers us the glorious vision of a united Church – one which fulfils Jesus' high priestly prayer, which receives the Father's commanded blessing, which confirms the Spirit's baptism into one body, and which causes the world to sit up and take note.

Simon Ponsonby, Pastor of Theology at St Aldates, Oxford

This book is profound, prophetic and heart-stirring. What is unity? Malcolm expounds scripture's answer. He reminds us that unity is something we already have, not something to strive for; it is something to maintain and to live from. This unity is a unity of love in which we love each other because Jesus first loved us, and we him; a unity based entirely on the relationship between heart and heart, a unity that is profoundly missional in its impact.

Stephen Ruttle, Senior Advisor to the Archbishop of Canterbury, trustee of New Wine, leading UK barrister and global leader in Mediation

Malcolm would love to hear your thoughts or stories of unity and invites you to connect with this subject on the Facebook Page "One for All" which can be found by searching @unitedforapurpose. He's keen to hear stories of what happens when churches work together and some of the challenges that this presents us with. He'd also love to learn from your stories and thoughts on unity.

Malcolm blogs at www.malcolmduncan.typepad.com, can be followed on Facebook at RevMalcolmDuncan, on twitter at @MalcolmJDuncan and can be contacted at malcolm.duncan@goldhill.org He'd love to connect with you.

One for All

THE FOUNDATIONS

The importance of unity
in a fractured world

MALCOLM DUNCAN

MONARCH
BOOKS
Oxford, UK & Grand Rapids, USA

Published by Monarch Books (an imprint of Lion Hudson plc)
Wilkinson House, Jordan Hill Road, Oxford OX2 8DR, England
Email: monarch@lionhudson.com www.lionhudson.com/monarch
and by Essential Christian, 14 Horsted Square, Uckfield TN22 1QG
Tel: 01825 746530 Email: info@essentialchristian.org Web: www.essentialchristian.org
Registered charity no 1126997'

ISBN 978 0 85721 810 0
e-ISBN 978 0 85721 811 7

First edition 2017

Acknowledgments

Unless otherwise indicated, Scripture quotations are from The New Revised Standard Version of the Bible copyright © 1989 by the Division of Christian Education of the National Council of Churches in the USA. Used by permission. All Rights Reserved.

Scripture quotations marked AMP taken from the Amplified® Bible, Copyright © 1954, 1958, 1962, 1965, 1987 by The Lockman Foundation. Used by permission.

A catalogue record for this book is available from the British Library

Printed and bound in the UK, March 2017, LH36

Contents

To the memory of my dear friend, brother and co-worker, Jim Graham – who demonstrated unity in how he lived and what he taught, and to our mutual friend, Charles Whitehead, whose life and witness continues to inspire me.

With heartfelt thanks and gratitude to Debbie, Matthew, Benjamin, Anna and Riodhna for your love, encouragement, and support – thank you your unstinting love and support.

Dedicated to all those who yearn for a greater unity in the body of Christ across the world.

Foreword

Public controversy and disagreement are now an everyday part of our culture. Social media like Facebook and Twitter permit and encourage people to express extreme views and to fall out over major issues of our time such that it feels that we're living in a world that is deeply divided. Whether it's President Trump denouncing all who criticise him as manufacturers of "fake news" or the deep rift between Remain and Leave supporters in and after the Brexit referendum, those divisions seem to colour the whole of our news and public debate.

But do Christians do any better? Not on the evidence of my email correspondence and social media timelines! People fall out pretty publicly on everything from traditional versus modern forms of worship to the leadership of women in church. As for my own church, the Church of England, you could be forgiven for thinking that the only preoccupation we have is how we deal with human sexuality and our acceptance (or lack of it) and pastoral care for lesbians and gay men, rather than our primary calling to the re-evangelisation of England.

Which is why *One for All* is timely. Malcolm Duncan goes to the very heart of some of the things that divide us. If we are to take Jesus' prayer in John 17 for his disciples (and those who succeed them – including us) seriously, what might it look like? It would be unity, not uniformity. It would include every Christian believer – none of us is exempt from the call to unity. It would be unity for the glory of the Father. It would be a unity which allows the Holy Spirit to work through each of us – and the whole Church – for the good of all.

One for All explores all this. Be prepared for some uncomfortable moments as God provokes you (and me) to think how we contribute to the scandal of disunity. Be prepared to be encouraged with good stories of people working together across divides. Be prepared to think how we might disagree well. And be prepared to be challenged by the amount of material in Scripture that challenges us to the calling of unity.

There are opportunities to reflect on the learning at the end of each chapter. This isn't necessarily a book to be read at one sitting – and it could well be used in discussion and bible study groups.

I'm glad that this has been our 2017 theme at *Spring Harvest*. Engaging practically, pastorally, and theologically with this – and encouraging other Christian festivals to do the same – can only be good for the whole Church here in the UK. So, now read on…

Pete Broadbent is Bishop of Willesden and Chair of the Essential Christian Board.

Acknowledgments

I f the old saying is true that it takes a village to raise a child, then it is equally true to say that it takes a team to write a book like this. I want to thank everyone involved in the journey of *One for All: The Foundations*. Particular thanks go to the Spring Harvest Planning Group and the Board of Memralife for your support and encouragement along the way. I am grateful to Peter Martin for his prayers and friendship. I am extremely grateful to the Spring Harvesters who show such love and support to me year by year – what a blessing it has been to lead you over these last five years. Thank you for your trust and love.

Thank you to those who have helped with the theological editing of the book. I am so grateful to you for your wisdom, your insight, and your guidance, particularly Stephen Holmes, Paula Gooder, Krish Kandiah, and Pete Broadbent.

Thank you also to the team at Lion Hudson who walk with me so faithfully and so patiently. Jenny Muscat, Nicki Copeland, Simon Cox, and Andrew Hodder-Williams – thank you for your faith in me, your encouragement, and your prayers.

Thank you to my wife, Debbie, and my four children, Matthew, Benjamin, Anna, and Riodhna, for your ongoing love, support, and care. I couldn't do this without you. I am also very grateful to Ellie, for her love, encouragement, and support – welcome to the family.

Thank you to the Gold Hill family and all those who are part of our wider church network – you are a blessing and I am thankful to God for you.

All of these people have walked with me through a difficult few years, when writing has been almost impossible, deadlines have been moved repeatedly, and life has been hard. Thank you so much for being patient, but more importantly for being kind.

Thank you to all who lead churches, whatever denomination or tribe they are from, who love Jesus and continue to press into His purposes and plans for the world. This book is for you: may it encourage and equip you.

Lastly, and most importantly, thank you to God, Whose faithfulness never ends, and Whose love is always enough.

Soli Deo Gloria.

Malcolm Duncan
Buckinghamshire
January 2017

Unity Matters

Where there is no enemy within, the enemies outside cannot hurt you.

Old African Proverb

The idea for this book was birthed in me in April of 2014 but its roots go further back than that. Spring Harvest is a large Christian festival that takes place in the United Kingdom every Easter. It attracts thousands of men, women, and children from across the country to come and enjoy good teaching, great worship, and some fantastic time together with other Christians. I have had the privilege of leading the Planning Group of the event since December 2012. Each year Christians from nearly all the denominations and streams arrive at Spring Harvest eager to meet with God and to make new friends. The event has been led brilliantly since it was birthed in the late 1970s by successive teams of men and women who long to see God's people encountering God, being inspired and resourced by that encounter, and becoming more confident and adventurous in their faith. It's a large event with up to 6,000 people gathering for each of the weeks we meet.

Before each Spring Harvest I try to spend a day or so with a small local church as I prepare for what lies ahead. It is my way of reminding myself that for most Christians the regular rhythm of their faith is lived in a small community. The average church congregation in the United Kingdom numbers in the low to mid-forties and in the United States of America it is not much higher.

So it was in April 2014 that I was driving from the Island of Bute in the Clyde Estuary in Scotland down through England to Minehead in North Somerset. I had led a church weekend at Rothesay Baptist Church on the island and was on my way to speak at Spring Harvest in the Butlins holiday camp at Minehead. The theme for the year was confidence in the gospel. We would be looking at the Apostles' Creed under the title, "Unbelievable: confident faith in a sceptical world".

Heading south, I was making my way through the beautiful scenery of Cumbria. I was enjoying the drive and thinking about the Spring Harvest event that was coming up when I sensed the Lord might be speaking to me. I remembered that it was on 31 October 1517 that Martin Luther had nailed his ninety-five theses to the door of the university in Wittenberg outlining his objections and concerns about the state of the Roman Catholic Church. So began the Reformation era.

Some people see that point in 1517 as a glorious moment of renewal and a new chapter in the story of God's purposes on the earth, and they celebrate the apparent rediscovery of grace and a perceived liberation of the Scriptures into the hands, the heads, and the hearts of ordinary men and women. Others see Luther's actions at Wittenburg as a moment of sadness and despair, when the church began to fracture in a painful and heartbreaking way that weakened her witness and divided her people. Whatever view you take, it was a watershed moment in the story of the church on the earth.

I began to think about the state of the church in the places around the world where I have ministered. I've had the privilege of preaching and teaching in almost sixty nations to all kinds of audiences. I've spoken in great and imposing cathedrals in Europe, mega-churches in the United States of America, under trees in Africa, and on rickety boats in Asia. As I thought about these different places, the simple question that came to my mind was this, "How united is the church in the world today?" I began to feel uneasy about the answer because, despite the wonderful things the church is doing and the utter beauty of the people of God around the world, I was very conscious that the scars of division and suspicion continue to mark us. I remembered the powerful words of Psalm 133 and the prayer of the Lord Jesus on the night before He was murdered, recorded in John 17:

> How very good and pleasant it is
> when kindred live together in unity!
> It is like the precious oil on the head,
> running down upon the beard,
> on the beard of Aaron,
> running down over the collar of his robes.
> It is like the dew of Hermon,
> which falls on the mountains of Zion.
> For there the Lord ordained his blessing,
> life forevermore.
>
> Psalm 133

"I ask not only on behalf of these, but also on behalf of those who will believe in me through their word, that they may all be one. As you, Father, are in me and I am in you, may they also be in us, so that the world may believe that you have sent me. The glory that you have given me I have given them, so

that they may be one, as we are one, I in them and you in me,
that they may become completely one, so that the world may
know that you have sent me and have loved them even as you
have loved me. Father, I desire that those also, whom you have
given me, may be with me where I am, to see my glory, which
you have given me because you loved me before the foundation
of the world."

John 17:20–24

Are we a united church?

As I reflected on these words I began to have a deep sense that Spring Harvest would have an important part to play in reminding the church across the United Kingdom of God's call upon us to be united. I reflected on the particular part of the church of the Lord Jesus to which I belong, the evangelical charismatic tribe. How good were we at being united? Did we display the grace, love, and patience of God with one another? I wasn't sure that we did. Was it possible that Spring Harvest could be used by God to help His people to stand together more intentionally? If it were to happen, then Spring Harvest would need to reach out to those in our part of God's family, the evangelical church in the United Kingdom.

It is true that Spring Harvest is a community where Christians from beyond the evangelical part of God's family meet others too, but we are predominantly an evangelical community and we are rooted in evangelical convictions theologically. Would it be possible for Spring Harvest to play a small part in reaching out to other Christians, affirming our unity first within the evangelical community, and then beyond that, could Spring Harvest do its part in standing with Christians from across the church in the United Kingdom? I began to sense the stirring of a prophetic purpose for Spring Harvest in 2017. Deep within my spirit I sensed that something was beginning to rise in our nation and around the world, and that God Himself was calling His people to remember that there is more that draws us together than pulls us apart. I believed that God could use an intentional statement of unity and commitment to a common cause in Christ to advance His Kingdom, but we would have to approach the issue with humility and a willingness to acknowledge our own weaknesses and failings. I remember thinking that the decision to explore the subject of unity would be uncomfortable for anyone involved. If we were to do it, God would expose our own failures to be agents of unity and He would remind us of our own belligerence.

How could we not explore such an issue, though? After all, evangelicals do not always have a strong reputation when it comes to Christian unity, despite the brilliant work of unity movements like the Evangelical Alliance.

So the idea of *One for All* was birthed. The Spring Harvest Planning Group talked about it and prayed about it and we believed that the Lord was asking us to explore the subject together. We also wanted to be part of something bigger, so with the help of other agencies and Bible weeks we began to discuss whether or not 2017 could be a year in which there were statements and commitments to unity across all the major evangelical festivals and Bible weeks in the United Kingdom. Those plans and discussions have resulted in a commitment by almost all the major Bible festivals in the UK, as well as some in other parts of the world, to declare that we are one in Christ, one in the gospel, and one for the sake of the world.

This book and its companion *One for All: The Implications* were birthed out of what God was saying to us in 2014.

I am not seeking to explore unity across faiths here. That is for another book. My central aim here is to explore what biblical unity means for evangelical churches. That is not to suggest that the only branch of Christianity that matters is the evangelical one, but rather to recognize that Spring Harvest, which is sponsoring the publication of this book and for whom the material is being written, is an evangelical community.

The material in this book and in the companion volume will be used by the 2017 Spring Harvest event itself, but it will also go further afield. By exploring the subject of evangelical unity I believe that the Spring Harvest community will be better placed to contribute to wider Christian unity, and surely wider Christian unity is a vital question for us to consider at this time. My prayer is that an evangelical church, strengthened in its own resolve to be united and committed to the gospel, to the Bible, and to Christ, will be a better and more effective contributor to wider Christian unity. It is as we understand ourselves as well as others that we can become more aware of what needs to change and what needs to remain the beating heart of our communities. Evangelicals are committed to the Bible, to the cross of Christ, to the centrality of conversion, and to being active and engaged in the world. So this book and its companion volume explore these key aspects of our identity under the lens of Christian unity.

In this volume I want to explore the biblical and theological foundations of unity by examining a few of the key Scriptures that talk about unity, namely the prayer of the Lord Jesus Christ in John 17, the words of Paul to the church in Ephesus at the beginning of Ephesians 4, and the words of the writer of Psalm 133. We will explore what biblical unity looks like and what Christ's prayer for unity means. These are important pillars upon which our conversations about unity and our reflections about what unity looks like can be built. The church rises or falls on our theology. Far too often we take the road of pragmatism at the expense of decent theological reflection. The result is a short termism that sustains us for a while but actually does us damage in the long run.

Much of what is said about unity is unhelpful. For example, when we make unity itself the goal, we will quickly run into problems. The Bible does not seem to make unity the goal of Christians in and of itself. Our unity is built around something. Our unity is for something. Our unity is not something that we strive for, but something that we protect and from which we live. The biblical and theological foundations of our unity are vital if we are to have healthy unity. Unity does not sacrifice truth. Unity does not scramble to the lowest common denominator but instead it flows out of the highest common commitment – Christ Himself. *One for All: The Foundations* explores these principles in more depth and seeks to create the skeleton upon which the flesh and sinews of practical unity can sit. This book is helpful for church leaders, pastors, network leaders, and those who want to think more biblically and theologically about unity and why it matters. Its aim is to take some time to reflect on the teaching of the three main biblical passages I have set out and tie them together in a way that provides a coherent underpinning of the practical implications of Christian unity.

The accompanying volume to this book is *One for All: The Implications*. Having done the hard theological work in this volume, I will turn our attention in the second work to what the implications of this unity might be. After a summary chapter at the beginning of the second volume, we will explore the following key questions about unity in *One for All: The Implications* in the light of the theological and biblical reflection of this volume:

1. How do we disagree well?

2. What could biblical unity across denominations and networks look like?

3. How do we respect human personhood in the midst of theological and spiritual disagreement?

4. What could unity across the generations look like?

5. How do we work together in mission and evangelism?

6. What does it mean for us to stand with persecuted brothers and sisters around the world?

As we approach these questions, I pray that we will do so with a great degree of humility and honesty. It would be true to say that unity is not the strongest card of the evangelical church but if we, as part of the wider body of Christ, are to become more effective for the Lord Jesus, we need to learn to get better at it.

Evangelicals are not always good at unity
– Martyn Lloyd-Jones and John Stott

It is quite sobering to read about the events of the great debate between two towering figures in British Evangelicalism that took place in October 1966. I am sure that both parties have been misrepresented and misunderstood, but nevertheless the exchange between these two giants of the evangelical world highlights some of the challenges faced by those of us in this part of the church when it comes to unity.

At an event facilitated by the Evangelical Alliance, Martyn Lloyd-Jones, the minister of Westminster Chapel in London, and John Stott, the rector of All Souls Church, Langham Place, also in London, clashed over the way ahead for British evangelicals. These two men were pulpit giants in an age when preaching seemed to be going out of fashion. There was then, as there is even more urgently now, a need to rediscover the centrality of preaching again. They each loved God deeply, loved the Scriptures, and loved the church. They were both leaders. They were both internationally renowned. Indeed, for many years a warm friendship existed between them personally and, without a doubt, both these men have had deep and lasting impacts on how we understand evangelicalism today. Stott represented the growing voice of Evangelicalism in the Anglican Community, and Lloyd-Jones the Evangelical wing of the Free Church. Yet they clashed very publicly and very passionately on 18 October 1966 on the issue of what the church was, what its purpose was, and how best to go about its mission. The dividing issues were the decisions and challenges being faced by evangelicals in the church in the United Kingdom.[1]

Lloyd-Jones wanted to see greater cooperation between evangelicals across denominations and church tribes. He argued that there should be a separation from the historic denominations and perhaps a new Evangelical Church denomination should begin. He was suspicious of the loss of identity, integrity, and purpose for evangelicals within the denominational structures in the United Kingdom. He believed that it was impossible to maintain a faithful witness for the long term in any denomination where its leaders had a broken understanding of the new birth.[2]

Stott did not see things in entirely the same way. As an evangelical Anglican, he believed that there were remarkable opportunities to strengthen the evangelical voice within the Anglican Church.

Their sharp disagreement can still be felt in some areas of the evangelical church today. One needs to look no further than the current wrestling within many denominations around the issue of sexuality to see how much of a challenge the idea of shaping a community around an evangelical heart actually is. Stott argued that it was the duty of evangelicals in the Anglican Church to remain. He said:

> Some evangelicals like myself, believe it is the will of God to remain in a Church that is sometimes called a "mixed denomination." At least until it becomes apostate and ceases to be a Church, we believe it is our duty to remain in it and bear witness to the truth as we have been given to understand it.[3]

This inherent conflict still exists within Evangelicalism. Stott undoubtedly won the day, but looking back over the fifty years since the debate in 1966, one cannot help but feel that both men were right and both men were wrong. Lloyd-Jones' desire for an evangelical church that could boldly and confidently proclaim the gospel is surely an attractive idea, but he became increasingly narrow in his definition of what that would look like. The great problem faced by the evangelical church is its constant tendency to disagree and subdivide, and by so doing to cut itself off from the world around us and from the broader Christian community.

Stott's dream of a renewed, reformed, and revitalized Anglican Church where the Thirty-Nine Articles would be given fresh passion, the gospel would be given fresh respect, and the church's structures, practices, and worldview would be repainted has failed to take place. While evangelicals in the Anglican Church are much more numerous now than they were fifty years ago, the Anglican family remains deeply divided over many key issues of doctrine and practice. In many ways, both Martyn Lloyd-Jones and John Stott were disappointed by where the church was heading.

We cannot underestimate the challenge of this core question: what is the purpose of the church? If we believe that it is to bring social change and transformation only, then a whole plethora of answers and avenues opens up before us. If it is to guard the gospel, then another series of roads stretch out ahead of us. If, however, the people of God are those who have experienced the grace of God through Christ and are now united in Christ and called to proclaim His gospel to the world around them in faithfulness and obedience, then the way ahead will look different again. In one sense, these questions of what the church is for and who we are sit at the heart of the discussion of unity. They are as vital now as they were in 1966. Does the church decide what makes us united or has God already united us and given us the task of protecting and guarding that unity?

Spring Harvest

Spring Harvest itself was born out of a desire to see evangelical Christians gather together and gain confidence through time spent with God and time spent with each other. The festival was birthed through the visionary leadership of Clive Calver and

Peter Meadows in the late 1970s and has continued to serve the evangelical church specifically and the wider church in general since that time.

However, Spring Harvest itself has not been free from controversy. Between 1993 and 2007 Spring Harvest partnered with a few other Christian organizations to deliver "Word Alive", an event that saw the largest number of evangelical students in Europe gathering together to explore Scripture, encounter God, and be equipped for mission in the world. By the middle of the 2000s, the Word Alive event was delivered by Spring Harvest and two other groups. However Word Alive and Spring Harvest parted company in the mid-2000s over a range of issues. "New Word Alive" was birthed and has been meeting annually since this time.

This separation had a deep impact on many within the evangelical community in the United Kingdom, and the pain it caused remained a cause for concern in the years following the separation. A beautiful and important journey of reconciliation has taken place in recent years, and the relationship between the two groups is stronger again. I have been blessed and encouraged by the friendship I have with the leader of the team that delivers New Word Alive. We have met and prayed together on a number of occasions. Indeed, both he and I have been very involved in discussions with the leaders of other evangelical agencies and festivals concerning how we can celebrate the things that unite us more publicly and more effectively. The events of the mid-2000s are, however, a painful reminder to me of the pain and heartbreak caused by division. All involved were godly leaders and the separation caused hurt on both sides. It was not the most glorious chapter of the story of evangelical unity from anyone's perspective.

When I became the chair of the Spring Harvest Planning Group in 2012, an interview with me was published in a leading Christian magazine in the United Kingdom. In that interview I was dismissive of the previous leaders of Spring Harvest. That was wrong of me and I regret it a very great deal. However unintentional it may have been, I offended and belittled my fellow leaders and I set a bad example. It sobers me to reflect on the fact that not only have I seen the pain caused by disunity but I have also contributed to it. How could I have allowed myself to be so foolish, and how did I manage to be so graceless and thoughtless? I jeopardized the very thing for which Spring Harvest had been established. If I were to have the ability to go back and re-record the interview I would certainly say things very differently. I never again want to be a contributor to schisms and factions in the church of Jesus Christ. If we take unity seriously then we must guard it. We must learn what it means to be quick to apologize and quicker to affirm our brothers and sisters.

Approaching the issue with humility

Evangelical Christianity has a propensity to become too comfortable with schisms. If we are not careful we can be too quick to reject those with whom we disagree in the name of purity and faithfulness. The result is a weakened witness with an ever-splintering spirituality. I was brought up in a family where Christianity was neither discussed nor practised. Having been converted in my mid-teens, I quickly became aware that Christianity in Northern Ireland was full of very strong views. Not all of these were wrong. I was taught many valuable lessons that remain with me today: a deep love of the Scriptures; the importance of remaining open to and always dependent upon the Holy Spirit; the centrality of prayer; the importance of evangelism and mission; the power of doctrine; the fickleness of emotions and of human nature; the radical call of the gospel to a forgiven and then a transformed life; the importance of gathering together; the blessing of consistent, regular giving; the call to holiness; the power of good preaching and teaching; the beauty of music and the arts. These and many other aspects of my Christian discipleship have proven themselves to be priceless to me.

Northern Ireland is an unusual place, though. I love it and thank God for it. The church in Northern Ireland has faced the most severe trials imaginable over many years. On both sides of the political and religious spectrum, too many mothers and fathers buried their sons and daughters because of the violence of "the other side". The culture of Northern Ireland is changing, thank God, but for a very long time it was a divided society, and the church often contributed to that division. In both the Roman Catholic and the Protestant communities in Northern Ireland there were deep senses of suspicion, injustice, and protectionism. Suspicion because our school systems were divided, our communities were divided, and our understanding of our culture was divided. Injustice because we all knew someone who had been murdered and we felt the wounds and the pain of the families left behind, and perhaps we quietly wondered if we, or someone we loved, would be next. Protectionism because an embattled community that feels threatened by those who surround it will always reach for certainties and sacred cows to protect. Trust isn't easy when you feel like you are in a war zone.

It is all the more remarkable, therefore, that I did not grow up in a sectarian home. Despite the fact that we lived in a strongly loyalist community, not one of my siblings or I ever became involved in paramilitary activity or sectarian activity. My mother and father were vehemently opposed to any sense of religious discrimination despite the fact that neither of them was particularly religious. They were christened into the Presbyterian Church in Ireland, as were all of us as children, but we did not attend church except for weddings, funerals, and christenings. Throughout my childhood, faith was irrelevant to the worth of a person or the contribution they could make to the community. I am proud of the courageous stance my parents took. They welcomed Roman Catholics into our home when others rejected them. My dad employed Roman Catholics despite threats to his own life. I even remember him helping neighbours who had been forced out of their homes because they were Roman Catholics.

When I became a Christian, however, I began to hear very different things. Thankfully the church I was part of was pretty balanced about such things, but there were those who had the conviction that being a Roman Catholic meant you could not possibly be a Christian. I had never heard that before I became a believer so I was shocked when I heard it afterward. Northern Ireland is the only country I know of where the term "interfaith dialogue" actually means discussions between the Protestant and Roman Catholic communities. Each community had a deep-seated suspicion of the other, and both sides of the community often lacked the humility to actually listen to the story of the other side. As a result, the watchwords of each toward the other were what I noted earlier, namely suspicion, injustice, and protectionism. It is always easier to build walls than it is to build bridges.

Having now lived outside Northern Ireland for about thirty years, I see the beauty and the resilience of the Christian communities there as well as the challenges. For every story of pain and heartbreak and division in my homeland, I know of other stories of hope and grace and transformation. Since leaving Northern Ireland I have had the privilege of being involved with wonderful Christian communities around the world. In every single situation where humility is evidenced, the beauty of Christ can be seen and the sense of Christian unity is strong. Where humility is not present, unity is almost impossible to experience. Humility prevents unnecessary division. It only takes an ounce of humility for us to recognize that we have often failed one another by being divided rather than united.

As we explore the principles and issues of unity, it is vital that we do so with an awareness of our own propensity to disunity. For us to be aware, we must know our own stories. I am still shaped by Northern Ireland. I am still shaped by being an evangelical. I am still shaped by finding my natural resting place in the Pentecostal and Baptist traditions of the church. It is as I acknowledge these preferences that I am enabled to prevent them becoming the pre-eminent definitions of who I am. Above these convictions and beyond these distinctive identities sits the most important definition of all – I am a Christian. Before I am Irish, before I am British, before I am a Pentecostal or an Evangelical or a Baptist, I am Christian. It is to the heart of this description that we should turn if we are to define what it means to stay united. We are united *in Christ* above and beyond any other thing. We are His first, and our link with each other flows from our link with Him. That's why we are brothers and sisters, and it is why being brothers and sisters is more important than almost anything else.

Reflection

How well do you know yourself and your own story? What do you think has shaped the way you think about unity? Think about the following areas of your history: your home life and its implications on how you understand unity; the cultural context in which you grew up and the way it has shaped your understanding of unity; the Christian context in which you came to faith and the denomination or denominations of which you are or have been part. What kind of an imprint have they left on you? There are bound to be some very positive impacts and some negative ones. Take some time to think about them.

How do you view the idea of evangelical unity? Does it appeal to you or do you reject it? In your own timeline think about the times when you have been the source of unity and the times when you have been the source of disunity. Is there anything you could do now to address those times when you contributed to disunity? What principles can you put in place in your life and ministry now to ensure that you protect and promote unity? Perhaps you could begin to think about a life charter or a small set of commitments you can make about how you conduct yourself so that you are someone who builds up unity. How will you use your position, your words, your influence, and your actions to promote and protect unity, and what will you do to address the areas of weakness in your character or outlook that contribute to disunity?

We're Family

"You can choose your friends, but you sho' can't choose your family, an' they're still kin to you no matter whether you acknowledge 'em or not, and it makes you look right silly when you don't."

Harper Lee, *To Kill a Mockingbird*[i]

I grew up in Northern Ireland as the youngest of five children. I had three brothers and one sister. Colin was twelve years older than me and died in March 2016. Edward is ten years older than me, Anne is almost eight years older than me, and Bill is just over six years older than me. Growing up in our home was an adventure! Our family started in the two-up and two-down houses of the Tiger's Bay area in North Belfast. After my parents married in the early 1950s they lived in one of these small houses in Canning Street. It was within walking distance of Harland and Wolff shipyard, where my dad worked as an electrician. My two eldest brothers were born there. Then in 1962 the family moved to a large council estate called Rathcoole. It sits about six miles north of Belfast in the borough of Newtownabbey and was built in the late 1950s to deal with the crisis in Northern Ireland that was created by the combination of extremely low-grade housing for the working class and a chronic lack of housing stock after the Second World War. At one point it was the largest social housing complex in Europe. It was there that my sister, my youngest brother, and I were all born.

My brothers and my sister were very good to me. I was a little spoiled by them, as I was the baby of the family. I love my family very much, but we can also drive one another mad on occasions. We can cut across one another, dismiss one another's opinions, and become annoyed with one another. We would often have Sunday lunch at the dining room table, with me perched on the middle of an ironing board that was stretched across two chairs to make a third chair for me, and we would argue, fight, and disagree. Of course, we all thought that our point of view was the right one and that everyone else was wrong. Sometimes, as our discussions got more and more heated, we would raise our voices. Growing up in our house was a hotbed of disagreement, discussion, and debate.

We all had different opinions on life, different ways of doing things, and different likes and dislikes. Looking back, I can honestly say that life was never dull. It wasn't always easy, but it was never boring! We all ended up doing very different things with our lives, too. Colin was a journalist. Edward is an engineer and electrician having also been a Royal Marine and a member of the French Foreign Legion (it's a long and complicated story!). Anne works with numbers as a credit controller. Bill is a lieutenant-colonel in the British Army. I ended up as a pastor and a theologian.

We also had times when our disagreements were more about seven people trying to share a house together. We got on one another's nerves. We used someone else's stuff without asking first. We forgot to let Mum know we weren't coming home for dinner. We turned up with friends without asking permission first. We left our dishes in the sink and our dirty washing on the floor. Living together as a larger family wasn't always easy. Money was tight, tempers were short, and emotions ran high.

There were also much more difficult things about growing up in my family. I didn't find it easy and I was sometimes very unhappy. We probably all were. At the end of the day, though, this was and is my family and I love them. As we grew up we might have criticized one another and fought; we might have fallen out with and upset one another; but when someone else attacked us, criticized us, or made harsh or unfair judgments about us, we linked arms and defended one another. You could criticize the family if you were a part of it, but there was no way we would let someone else run us down or tear us apart. The unspoken motto in our house as we were growing up was that we were family and we were stuck with each other. Good or bad, happy or mad, we shared blood. In the words of Harper Lee, we could choose our friends, but we couldn't choose our family.

I am not sure that there is such a thing as a "broken" family. Family is family. It is not determined by a marriage certificate alone or a decree absolute or an adoption order. Families begin and end in the commitments we make to one another in our hearts. The only time when family becomes null and void is when the ties in our hearts are cut off. When we cut those ties, or someone else does, then the people around us cease to be our family. That can be devastating. Even if we hate those ties, though, if we do not cut them off then those people are still our family. My three living siblings and I are all now adults. We still disagree. We still do things that irritate one another. We've been through some pretty heartbreaking stuff together. Our life together has been tempered by suffering's heat, shaped by circumstances, and beaten by adversity's hammer. Distance from one another has at times been a blessing and at times a great curse. Through it all, though, family is family. We haven't given up on each other and we don't intend to.

The church is one family

Despite the vastness of the church, we are still one family. There are around two billion Christians in the world. That amounts to about one-third of the world's population. Approximately 36,000 different denominations and Christian streams exist today that are divided into five big blocks of believers. There are in the region of one billion Roman Catholics and around 400 million Protestants. Approximately 220 million believers are part of the Orthodox Church, 85 million Christians describe themselves as Anglicans, and somewhere in the region of 275 million would use the label "Independent" to describe their Christian religious convictions.

Yet there is one church; not five churches, not 36,000 churches, but just one church. Paul's challenge to the believers in Ephesus calls us to reflect on the implications of that reality:

> *I therefore, the prisoner in the Lord, beg you to lead a life worthy of the calling to which you have been called, with all humility and gentleness, with patience, bearing with one another in love, making every effort to maintain the unity of the Spirit in the bond of peace. There is one body and one Spirit, just as you were called to the one hope of your calling, one Lord, one faith, one baptism, one God and Father of all and through all and in all.*
>
> Ephesians 4:1–6

Unity affects us all

Unity among Christians is a much bigger issue than just how congregations and denominations relate to one another. It is about how families work, how Christian friends talk to one another, how charities and businesses run by Christians or run for the glory of God function, and how we treat one another both privately and publicly. It's about the way we use words on social media and in the press. Unity is about how we view one another, treat one another, and think of one another all the time. Unity is a heart issue. Protecting it should be one of our highest priorities.

Having been a pastor for more than half of my life, I've seen the impact of disunity on churches, organizations, and families. The devastation that takes place when relationships break down is heartbreaking. I've seen the impact of lies, jealousy, deceit, affairs, fear, resentment, and a dozen other poisons as they eat into the lives of beautiful people and destroy them. I've stood in the pulpit and watched people who can barely talk to one another sit beside each other in a church service. I've knelt at my prayer stool and wept for men and women whose lives have been laid waste by a break in a relationship with someone they loved, worked with, or trusted. I've even buried people and had to try to help loved ones who left it too late to sort out a feud. Whether a division is over money, power, hurt, refusal to forgive, or anger, the impact of disunity and division is awful. It leaves a terrible legacy of apprehension, suspicion, and isolation, and it can take years to recover from.

There has to be a better way of relating to one another. God does not want His people to look at one another suspiciously. He did not make us to build fences and to hide ourselves away from one another. He wants us to be one. There is enough suspicion, attack, and criticism outside of the church without us bringing it inside as well. What is the solution? If we want the church to do better at unity, we need to work out how to help those of us who are part of it to be more like Jesus and to treat one another the way He would.

Principled unity

Amid the great challenges that the church in the world faces today it is inevitable that there will be disagreements among us as well as strong arguments between us. Any healthy family needs to grapple with what it means to be a family while at the same time knowing how to disagree with one another. This is not to be feared and it is most certainly not to be shied away from. A unity that fears the truth or avoids honest conversation is fatally flawed from the outset.

We do not have to be the same to be united. We can disagree without dividing. A failure both to wrestle with the truths of Scripture and to seek the mind of the Spirit results in an emaciated church that is nothing more than a pale reflection of the culture around us. Christian unity is built upon the truth of who God is, what He does through Christ, and how He has revealed Himself to us through Christ as displayed in the Scriptures and interpreted by the church through the years. We are not free to change these realities. We are not free to craft a different Jesus or to change the Scriptures according to our preferences or desires.

Truth matters in Christian unity. In fact, a commitment to truth is the wellspring of Christian unity, not the result of it. That probably means that there are some issues that we feel so passionately about that they lead to our separation, but even in separation we can treat one another with love and grace. We do not have to destroy one another when we disagree. Inevitable disagreements notwithstanding, we still have to work out how to love one another.

The New Testament shows us a church facing the threat of division

There is nothing new under the sun. Disagreement in the church is as old as the church itself. In fact, most of the letters in the New Testament were written to address issues of division and disagreement and to guide the church on the road to maturity. The New Testament bristles with issues that could have permanently divided the body of Christ. Beginning with the complaints of the early church about a lack of care for some believers as recorded in Acts 6, we can trace a journey of potential division across the pages of the New Testament. We see these threats in the spiritual arrogance, personality cults, and sexual sins of Christians in Corinth; the legalism of Christians in Galatia; the gossip and backbiting of believers in Philippi; the obsession with angels in the minds of the followers of The Way in Colossae; the pressures of life for Christians in Rome; misunderstandings about the second coming for Christians in Thessalonica; slavery and its implications for Philemon; persecution for the Christians to whom Peter addressed his general epistles; or the looming threat of Rome for those to whom John addressed the book of Revelation, not to mention the theological and pietistic divisions and suspicions in the seven letters of Jesus at the beginning of the last book of the Bible. The threat of division was real and present from the beginning of the church's life. The New Testament has answers to the questions of how to maintain unity and how we avoid division. The issue is not a new one and the answers are not new either. We will find help in the pages of the Bible if we want to stay united.

There are many challenges to unity today

There are real dangers for the church today too. We face division and separation over a number of issues. The role of women continues to be a challenge for many, with a number of churches holding the view that women cannot hold positions of leadership or preach and teach while others embrace the ministry of women in any and all areas where a woman believes God has called her.

The issue of sexuality threatens to split a number of denominations as some Christians believe that men or women who are in active same-sex relationships should be welcomed into the church without challenge and should be free to minister wherever a call is affirmed while others believe that such a lifestyle is contrary to the teaching of the Bible and therefore cannot be endorsed.

The distinctiveness of Yahweh is an issue for some leaders, with some Christians believing that the Allah of Islam is simply another form of description for the God of the Jews and Christians while others believe that Allah and Yahweh are completely different in character, nature, and purpose.

What we do with the Bible is a vital and challenging issue for many. Is it the inspired and infallible Word of God or not? What do "inspired" and "infallible" actually mean? Are there parts of the Bible that are irrelevant today? How central should it be in our preaching and life, and what does it actually mean to be biblical?

There are huge discussions and potential rifts in the church over the nature of worship, the way in which we disciple people, and even what the gospel is. What does it mean to be a follower of

Jesus? Does evangelism still matter? What is the gospel? How do we do mission? What constitutes a church? Does church discipline still matter? What are the main responsibilities of a pastor? How does authority work in the church? The list of areas of potential division is an extensive one.

Learning to disagree well

These challenges, debates, and areas of potential conflict are neither imaginary nor theoretical. Their impact is felt in families where these issues land. There is a mother or a daughter who believes she is called to preaching and leadership but a father or brother who disagrees. Pastoral conflicts are taking place in a number of churches over people who experience same-sex attraction and their place in the local church. Leadership teams are wrestling with what it means to hold a clear biblical line while being compassionate and pastoral at the same time. Denominations are facing strain because their member churches are looking for leadership and feel like they are not getting it, or they are looking for freedom and feel like they are getting leadership that is too centralized and too directive. Anglicans are struggling with the shape of shared conversations on human sexuality, with some leaders feeling they are moving too slowly, others feeling they are moving too fast, and still others believing that the outcome is a foregone conclusion.

In all of these potential rifts and divisions, people still matter. Their sense of identity, purpose, calling, significance, and worth are affected by the outcomes of the various discussions and debates. On the face of it, there seems to be ample evidence to suggest that we are not as good at diversity as the early church was, and we seem to struggle with others who have a different view to us more than the New Testament writers did. We feel much more ready to part ways than the church did in the first 100 years of its history. It is worth remembering that throughout the New Testament, with all of the divisions and dissentions that were being addressed, the writers maintained the view that the recipients of their words were still their brothers and sisters. Deep disagreement was held in tension with a ready willingness to see the person with whom they disagreed as part of the family.

It feels like we have more orthodoxy tests than they did and a lower threshold of tolerance than they had. Why are we so quick to proclaim that someone with whom we disagree is not a Christian? Maybe it is because we see our role as protecting the truth. Perhaps in order to protect the truth we sometimes fall into the traps of the Pharisees of Jesus' day? We see ourselves as right and everyone else as wrong. We define the truth in ever narrowing terms because we do not want to dilute it. We create our own litmus tests of orthodoxy (right worship and doctrine) and orthopraxy (right behaviours), believing that by doing so we are maintaining faithfulness to the gospel and to the Bible. We ostracize and reject those who are in a different camp. We are dismissive of new thinking.

All of these actions and reactions flow from a deep desire to honour God, honour the work of Christ, and honour the Bible. The Pharisees wanted to do these things too but unwittingly became a group that excluded so many in the name of faithfulness. We must be careful not to do the same thing while at the same time seeking to honour God, the gospel, the Bible, and the distinctive life and calling of the church. It is not easy, because how we handle disagreements and discussions is as vital as the subjects themselves.

We must not pretend that every view has equal biblical validity because that is simply logically and philosophically incoherent. It may be difficult, but it is right to point out that if someone claims to be biblical but contradicts the plain teaching of Scripture then they are, quite simply, wrong. Equally, we must not behave as if we are always right and everyone else is always wrong. Somehow we must learn the art of biblical humility alongside biblical confidence if we are to protect any sense of meaningful unity. We must learn what it means to disagree well.

One place in the early church that provides us with an object lesson in the importance of unity and how to protect it is the city of Carthage.

Lessons from Carthage

In the second and third centuries after Christ, North Africa was a province of the Roman Empire with Carthage as its capital. Part of the same area today is Tunisia. All roads may have led to Rome, but many of them passed through Carthage. The city was known as the granary of the Roman Empire and it was a bustling centre of trade, art, culture, and food. It was also a cradle of Latin theology for the emerging church. It was a hotbed of emerging ideas. It is no surprise, therefore, to discover that it was an area where there were strong disagreements in the church. How those disagreements were handled is of immense importance to us today as we seek to grapple with disagreement. There are lessons for the importance of unity in the family of God for us in Carthage if we will look. Let me introduce just three principles about how we relate to one another in the church that we can learn from the Christians in Carthage.

1. Remember that the world is watching

One of Carthage's great Christian fathers was Tertullian (c. AD 160–220). He was raised in a non-Christian family and well educated in Latin grammar, rhetoric, and philosophy. His pathway to becoming a lawyer or a leading civil servant seemed set. Tertullian converted to Christianity, however, and eventually became one of the leaders of the church in Carthage. He was the first major theologian to write in Latin, beginning the challenging task of translating a written and received truth from one tradition and culture to another. He was an apologist,[5] which, put simply, means that he set out to present a defence of Christianity to the society and the culture around him. He saw the best defence of Christianity as a good offence. In his works, *To the Gentiles* and *Apology*, he argued that pagan beliefs and practices were wrong and that the Christian life, as taught in the Scriptures and modelled in the church, was right. Tertullian imagined that those outside the church would look at the church and be challenged by how Christians loved one another because non-Christians did not share this deep commitment to their fellow human beings. He believed that as non-Christians saw that Christians were willing to die for one another, the non-Christians would be challenged. In other words, Tertullian argued that the deep love, commitment, and affection of Christians for one another would stand out in a culture of suspicion and selfishness. This argument was the basis of Tertullian's famous phrase, "Behold how they love one another," referring to the powerful witness of mutual love and respect in the Christian community. His actual words were,

Look... how they love one another (for they themselves [pagans] hate one another); and how they are ready to die for each other (for they themselves are readier to kill each other).[6]

Among many things, Tertullian reminds us of the need for the church to be a community of love, grace, and support for one another, and he challenges us to remember that the world is watching how we behave toward one another. It is horrifying to see the way Christians talk about one another in full gaze of the wider public. One only has to read through some of the comments that appear on social media websites such as Facebook and Twitter when a controversial issue is being discussed between Christians to realize just how poor our witness can be in this area. We say things in those contexts that we would never dream of saying if we were face to face with someone. Tertullian spoke of a world that saw how Christians loved one another and were impacted by the depth of that love and mutual care. While this is still often true of Christians today, it is increasingly possible to see the very opposite in the world of public discourse between Christians. The world watches how we tear one another apart and wonders how there could be any truth to the claim that we serve a God of love and grace. We simply must remember that the world is watching what we say and how we say it.

2. There is only one church and we must not be authors of division

The second great leader of the church in Carthage was Cyprian (c. AD 200–258). He, like Tertullian, was converted to Christianity in his adult years. He was trained as an orator but eventually became the Bishop of Carthage.

Just after becoming the Bishop of Carthage, Cyprian faced a crisis. Decius, the Roman Emperor (AD 249–251), demanded that all Roman citizens perform a public sacrifice to the gods of the Roman Pantheon. While many Christians refused to do this, some did perform the sacrifice. Cyprian went into hiding and continued to lead the church, but he had to address the question of what to do with those believers who sacrificed to the gods of the Roman Pantheon but then sought to repent of their error and have fellowship with the believers again.

Novatus was a leader of the church in Carthage who refused to sacrifice to the Roman gods. He was imprisoned for his refusal and he claimed that his suffering gave him the right and the authority to forgive those who had sacrificed and were now repentant. Cyprian called for a Council to be held in Carthage in AD 251 but Novatus and his supporters continued to issue letters of pardon and forgiveness. The church in North Africa faced a schism over the issue. Cyprian's address to the Council in Carthage in AD 251 was entitled *On the Unity of the Catholic[7] Church* and has survived the years. Rather than focusing on the issue of whether or not to forgive and restore the lapsed believers, he addressed the division that Novatus' actions were creating in the church.

Cyprian argued that the devil wages an external war on the church through persecution but that the most dangerous wars he wages are around issues of schism and division. Cyprian said the greater issue of division must be addressed before the issue of forgiveness for the lapsed could be addressed. He argued that although the church is made up of many congregations, there is only one church. He compared the church to the sun. Although there are many beams of light from the sun, there is only one sun:

The Church, bathed in the light of the Lord, spreads her rays throughout the world yet the light everywhere diffused is one light and the unity of the body is not broken.[8]

This concept of one church would, in the years between Cyprian's ministry and now, come to be the underpinning of the idea that there was no true and faithful church outside of the Roman Catholic Church or outside of those denominations and streams of the church that could trace their lineage back to the apostles themselves. The exclusivity of such a position and its implications challenges many people, like me, from a non-conformist and non-episcopal standpoint. There are many people who would argue that a different form of church government or organizational structure, or a different approach to liturgy and worship, are more than possible within Christ's global family without breaking the unity of the church. We do not have to throw the idea of the inherent unity of the church out with the bathwater of our denominational distinctiveness. One can hold to Cyprian's conviction about the unity of the church without accepting the implication that there should be one church government. The reality is that there is only one believing church in the world today, made up of *all* those who belong to Christ from whatever tribe, stream, and denomination they have found their way into. Not only that, but it is more than possible to accept that there are many who are part of the church in its outward expressions but who are not yet part of the believing body of Christ. God Himself will separate the goats from the sheep, the tares from the wheat. Beyond these tricky theological and ecclesiological questions, however, lies the foundational assumption that there is only one church and that it is the body of Christ. Would anyone suggest Christ has two bodies on earth?

We must be careful not to allow our denominational distinctiveness to become a denominational barrier. I would argue that there is great beauty in the diversity of the church. There are many forms and ways of gathering, making decisions, worshipping, preaching, and organizing ourselves. Millions of Christians feel most at home in Baptist churches around the world while millions of others enjoy the form and personality of the Pentecostal churches. Those who are part of the Anglican Communion enjoy the style and approach of that church family across its many expressions. This diversity can be a gift, providing space and freedom to people from different backgrounds, personality types, and temperaments. When we make this diversity a barrier to recognizing the validity and inclusion of another person we fall into difficult ground. Not everyone has to be a Baptist to be a Christian, nor does every believer have to be an Anglican or a Roman Catholic!

3. The greatest of sins is to hate a brother or a sister

The third leader of the church in Carthage for us to consider is Augustine of Hippo (AD 354–430). Viewed by many as the greatest theologian of the church since Paul and by others as a blight on the life and witness of the church, Augustine also had to deal with issues of division and unity in the church. One of his great challenges was the Donatist schism.

The Roman emperor Diocletian (AD 244–311) initiated what many consider to be the first general persecution of the church, sometimes called the Great Persecution (AD 303–305).

He demanded that Bibles and other sacred books should be burned. Some leaders handed over the sacred texts and were called *traditores*,[9] from which we get the word "traitor". The persecution ended and those leaders who had given up their Scriptures wanted to continue as priests. The issue that the church then faced was simple: does a leader's administration of the sacraments become invalid when the leader has been unfaithful to God?

Donatus believed that the purity of a leader's administration of the sacraments depended on the leader's moral purity. His argument was winning ground in North Africa. Augustine disagreed. He shared Cyprian's view of the unity of the church. Augustine believed God was the power behind the sacraments, not the church leader, because God Himself is the source of our hope and faith, not a leader. Augustine argued that we are deeply connected to one another as Christians because of who God is and what God has done for us in Christ. He used Romans 5:5 as a strong basis for this argument:

> God's love has been poured into our hearts through the Holy Spirit that has been given to us.
>
> Romans 5:5

Augustine could not fathom the possibility that division was right. He saw the Donatists as promoting division. He argued that Christians should remain united and continue to love one another in spite of their differences until those differences were resolved. In other words, Augustine argued that Christians were to choose unity over division. Only by this strong commitment would the love of the Spirit eventually force out the divisions between Christians and bring harmony within the church. He argued that the Donatists were forcing schism and division because other Christians were not living up to their self-imposed standards. Augustine saw the Donatists as committing a sin that no true Christian can commit – hatred for a brother or a sister. The issue was finally resolved at the council of Carthage in June AD 411, when Augustine's arguments won the day. Augustine was absolutely resolute in arguing that whatever differences exist between Christians, even in doctrine, they should not divide Christians.

Today, division is often the easy option, but it is seldom the best option. There are, no doubt, issues upon which we must take a stand and which themselves define the very use of the word "Christian". These issues are often the areas in which the culture of the day is most opposed to the teaching of the Bible. Upon these issues the church must take a stand, because failure to do so would weaken our understanding of the gospel itself. So it is no surprise that the issues of human personhood such as gender, sexuality, and race have generated so much discussion, raised so many passions, and led to such heated exchanges as they have. Yet if division does occur over these issues, as well it may, then such division itself must be seen as a heartbreaking result of our inability as Christians to reach a shared viewpoint. Unity at any cost should not be an option, but division is always a painful decision and is itself proof of the fallen nature of people. If we love one another, division will always be painful, even when it is the only way forward that we can see.

The challenges for us

There is nothing new under the sun. Tertullian reminds us that the world is still watching. He explored how to live the Christian faith in a culture and society that neither accepted nor welcomed it.

Cyprian reminds us that the church is one and it is wrong to be the author of division. He defended the organic unity of the church despite emerging factions and arguments, and he reminded the believers that they were to make loving one another the highest priority. Augustine reminds us of the need to love one another even in the midst of our doctrinal disagreements. He argued that we must not give up on one another. He sought to show that faithfulness to the Scriptures was vital for the believer and that the greatest sin was that of hatred of another Christian. Indeed, Augustine would argue that such hatred was evidence that the one doing the hating was not a Christian at all.

The church in North Africa faced persecution and pressure and as a result made mistakes. In the wake of those mistakes, believers had to wrestle with issues of forgiveness, restoration, and trust. All three leaders of the church in Carthage made clear that unity should be protected and given the highest possible priority. They did not argue for unity at the expense of truth but instead they held out for unity that wrestled with truth. If division were to happen, it would happen with broken hearts. Disunity was never the first option; it was only the last resort.

We are part of a church that has divided so many times that we almost think it is the norm. We have allowed ourselves to make secondary issues primary sources of division while we have allowed primary issues to go unaddressed. We have ignored the example and the advice of Tertullian, Cyprian, and Augustine. Winning an argument has often become more important than loving a brother or sister. Some of us have taken on the mantle of Donatus, declaring ourselves as the arbiters and interpreters of truth. We have allowed our understanding of the Scriptures to become the only possible understanding of the Scriptures. It is true that some areas of the Bible's teaching are crystal clear and that to claim otherwise is to undermine the Bible itself. On these issues we must take a stand, because when a person's view of a secondary issue challenges the authority of the Bible then the issue becomes one of primary importance. Where the Scriptures are clear we must be clear, even if it means we are culturally unpopular.

Others of us have allowed the truth to become an unimportant detail, a mere dot above an "i" or a line across a "t". We have embraced relativism in the name of contextualizing the gospel, but by so doing we have mistakenly diluted the gospel rather than contextualizing it. Some of us have stepped into the modern shoes of Novatus. We have allowed our "issue" to become more important than the unity of the body. We have placed our conviction on a specific issue, such as sexuality, above the issue of protecting the unity of the church. Such narrowing of focus and hardening of position has taken place on both sides of the debates around sexuality. We have allowed our desire to win that argument to outstrip our commitment to love one another. What we see in the New Testament church and in the church as it emerged in North Africa was a relentless commitment to love one another, an awareness of the need to pull the issues of the day into and under the implications of the truth, and a constant awareness that the wider world was watching the way they talked and behaved.

If only we could hold these same principles in our minds as we address the issue of unity in the church. Perhaps we can?

Reflection

Tertullian, Cyprian, and Augustine are historical figures who teach us a great deal about how we behave toward one another as Christians. Take some time to think about whether your witness and the witness of the local church that you are part of and the church in your town send a message that you love one another. Are there times when you speak badly of one another across the church in your area? What could you do about that? How could you take the initiative so that unity becomes something you place at the top of the agenda in your area? Are there things that would be better to be done together that you are currently doing separately? Have your denominational differences become too important in your area or in your own thinking? While you might hold to them very strongly, how can you make sure that you celebrate the things that you hold in common with other Christians above that which divides you? Has your local church ever closed its doors so you could join together with other Christians in the area or do you always expect them to close so that they can come and join you? What resources can you share? Lastly, think about the areas where division feels unavoidable. How will you disagree well? What can you do to make sure that in taking a stand for the truth you do not damage the witness of the church? Are you sure that the issues upon which you are dividing are foundational and rooted in truth and are not just preference? If division is unavoidable, how can you ensure that your separation is done in such a way that the world still sees your humility and that you are motivated by love, grace, and truth?

God's Plea

I cannot begin to express to you how important I think the issue of unity is for the church in the world today. Without it we have little or nothing to say to the world around us. I cannot find the words that are necessary to articulate the cry of my heart for us to stand together. I am utterly convinced that when we stand together and serve together we are stronger together. Rather than try to find my own arguments, I want to present to you the pleas of some of the Bible's writers as they reflected on the importance of unity. I have drawn together some of the words prayed or spoken by Jesus and some of the words written by Paul, John, Matthew, Peter, and one of the psalmists, and I have crafted a plea for unity that I believe represents their heart and their yearning.

The letter that follows is not a word-for-word translation of their words but I do believe it resonates with their yearning for Christ's church to be one. The Scriptures I have interpreted are themselves inspired of God and so they echo God's own heart cry, articulated through the original authors of these words, for unity and togetherness. The issue of our relationship with one another is deeply important to God and should, therefore, be deeply important to us. It is the cry of my own heart to each of us that we might give ourselves to being one.

Each section of the letter is my own interpretative paraphrase of specific passages of Scripture that I have crafted together. The original excerpts are detailed in the endnotes. The original authors capture the yearning of God's heart that we might be one. May we hear that passion as we read these words, and may we reflect on what each of us can do to preserve and protect the unity of the body of Christ.

To every single brother and sister in Christ

I am pleading with you with all the passion, intensity, and authority that Jesus has given me and because we are each under His Lordship and therefore irrevocably connected to one another. I beg you to recognize that you need to be united and to stick together, affirming and acting upon the principle that you should not allow any schisms, divisions, or factions to develop between yourselves. Instead, I urge you to be committed to standing shoulder to shoulder and acting together with a shared and single-minded determination and purpose.[10]

Different roles don't mean we need to have different agendas. It is true that God has designed us with distinct roles and responsibilities by making some of us people who start new things with vision and passion because of the resurrected Jesus; giving some of us the ability to share His heart in a powerful way, both for what is happening now and what will happen in the future; gifting some of us with a passion to reach people who are not yet followers of Jesus with the incredibly positive, powerful, and life-transforming message of who Jesus is and why He came; and enabling some of us to shepherd those God entrusts to us by protecting them, guiding them, instructing them – tenderly, clearly, and strongly – and setting them an example in our own priorities and conduct. All these roles combine with one clear, united aim and purpose, though, which is to prepare, train, and release Christ's holy followers to get on with the task of serving God by serving His powerful purposes in the world. Whatever our role might be, we are all called to demonstrate Christ's values and priorities by living as His servants ourselves, and to give our energy and passion to strengthening, increasing, and honouring Christ's very body on earth, the family of God that we call the church. We are to persevere at this magnificent task until the unity that He has given us in principle is clearly demonstrated in the way we think, the way we behave, and the way we treat one another.

This unity is deeply embedded in the truth of who Jesus is and what He has done, and in the purposes of God for us. The more clearly we understand Jesus and the closer we come to who He is, why He came, and what He has done, the more powerfully we will demonstrate this principle of standing together and serving together. That is because we will fundamentally understand that because of who the Son of God is and what He has done for us, we are immeasurably stronger together than we are on our own. As we step into this powerful unity we will learn to straighten our backs and walk with greater confidence and courage, looking resolutely into the world around us with the same boldness of heart and gravitas as our Saviour Himself did.[11]

It is as clear as the nose on one another's faces that we need each other. The different parts of a body have different functions to fulfil but they are all needed. The same is true of us. If we forget that we will never stay united.[12]

It is not always easy to get along, so we have to learn to put up with one another, and we can only do that with God's help. Putting up with one another means we have to learn to first allow God to work through us, then we have to learn the art of standing together and getting along better. That means that even when someone has a legitimate reason for being unhappy with someone else in the family we have to deal with it properly and learn what it means to cancel the debt caused by the situation and be gracious, kind, and forgiving toward one another.

The foundation for that course of action is to simply remember that you need to learn to treat other people the way Jesus has treated you. He has been gracious, kind, and compassionate to you and cancelled your debt to Him by forgiving you. The incredible flow of His forgiveness to you is not supposed to stop with you; it is supposed to flow through you to one another. This is not an optional extra. It is a fundamental part of being in God's family. To make this way of life a priority, you need to dress yourself in unconditional, accepting, and welcoming love. That is the same kind of love that Jesus has shown to you. Only that kind of love can hold you together as God's people. Without it you will sound like an orchestra that is out of tune, but with it you will make the most remarkable and attractive sound together. With this kind of love the symphony of your lives will be utterly faultless and you will sound pitch-perfect to a world that is yearning for good music.[13]

This sense of being a deeply united family is the heartbeat of what Jesus Himself asked His Father for. His prayer for this is breathtaking in its scope. He didn't only want this kind of togetherness for those who were His contemporary followers;

He also wanted it for those of us who have come into the family and acknowledged Jesus as our Lord and our Head because of the words that His contemporaries have spoken. Our spiritual life and priorities flow directly from Jesus' contemporary followers and we therefore share their spiritual DNA. That is why we feel the impact of His prayer. Jesus wants us all to be united, to be one family. He doesn't want a single one of His family to be left out. There is no one anywhere in the family of God who should feel isolated, cut off, or as if they are not part of His body.

The unity and singleness of heart, mind, and purpose Jesus wants for us has its deep roots in who God Himself is. The relationship between Jesus and His Father is the source and the symbol of the kind of relationships that Jesus wants us to have with God and with one another. The roots of our lives need to be deeply embedded in who God is, what God has done for us, and what He wants to do among us and through us. And the purpose of this togetherness and unity is absolutely clear.

It isn't just so we can be happy. Our unity and togetherness is not an end itself. Our unity, togetherness, and singleness of heart demonstrate to the world around us that Jesus was who Jesus claimed to be. Our unity is a magnet that draws people to Jesus and is one of the core ways in which the world around us comes to understand that Jesus truly is the Messiah, the Saviour of the world, and that the Father sent Him to the world to rescue, redeem, and renew us.

The astounding thing is that Jesus has already given us the very same splendour and brilliance that He enjoys with His Father. It is not something that He plans to give us at some point in the future. He has already given it to us. That glorious, shimmering brilliance is like a magnet that draws us to one another, and the closer we come to one another, the more brightly we shine. The gift of His glory in us has a knock-on effect. This gift to us is supposed to make us increasingly realize that we are already connected to one another. Our practice of unity has to follow the reality of the gift of unity we have already been given.

The more brightly we shine, the more attractive we appear to others. Actually, what is attractive to others is the brilliance and the shimmering beauty of Jesus in us individually and, more powerfully, in us collectively. Jesus reiterates this reality forcefully for us as He prays. He wants us to understand and be shaped by the abiding and constant reality that He has already given us His presence. It is His presence rather than simply our effort that is the basis of our shared life, shared identity, and shared purpose. Our unity is nothing more and nothing less than a mirror of the unity between the Father and the Son. His gift of unity to us is utterly comprehensive, impacting every single part of our understanding of ourselves, of others in the family, and of our place and purpose in the world around us.

God has done it this way for a reason. He wants the world around us to see beautiful, purposeful, life-giving relationships and to realize that He Himself is beautiful, purposeful, and life-giving. As the world around us sees this kind of common life and common purpose it is drawn toward the reality that God has a common life and common purpose and has shown it to us in sending the Lord Jesus to the earth. As they see this they realize that it is love that sits at the heart of God's character and actions. Love unites the Father and the Son. The same love unites God and His people. The same love unites His people with one another. The same love flows from His people to those who are not yet His people.[14]

The beauty of such unity automatically captures the attention of others. It is dazzlingly attractive and inherently good. It has a positive and affirming impact on those who see it. It has an even greater impact on those who experience it. It can be enjoyed in the same way as the beautiful scent of a garden that is full of different flowers. Such a garden can produce a magnificent and attractive aroma. To put it another way, it can be experienced like the wonderful atmosphere at a party where there are lots of different people yet everyone is having fun. Alternatively, it can be tasted in the same way that all the ingredients that go into a beautiful meal can be when they combine to make one unforgettable tasting experience. The challenging thing is that flowers take time to grow together, friendships and relationships develop over different shared experiences, and the best-tasting meals take time to cook so that the flavours can mingle together slowly.

The same is true of the unity that God has given us. Although it is His gift to us, it becomes more visible to others and more enjoyable to all the longer we ourselves enjoy it, commit to it, and live in it. As we give it our time and attention, this sense of common purpose, common identity, and common heart becomes like an incredibly attractive cologne or perfume that has drenched us. I'm not talking about a little hint of the scent here and there. I mean it feels like the whole bottle has been poured over us and the scent is infusing the air both far and wide. Such a committed and consistent approach to unity soaks those who experience it with life, refreshment, and vitality. It's like a daily deluge of God's provision and blessing, like a mist of mercy or a staggering, breathtaking sunrise of grace for all who experience it. When we live in the reality of this gift of unity we experience a continual sense of blessing, life, peace, and purpose. Not only that, the world around us also experiences the same powerful benefits.[15]

These immense benefits of unity are the bedrock of why we need to make it a central principle of our own lives both individually and together. We need to make it a priority to have relationships that go beyond superficiality and instead develop habits and attitudes that are conduits for the unity God has already given us. We share life together, not just meetings, because we share a common purpose, a common identity, and a common destiny. We are in this thing called "life" together. We are in God's family together. We endure hardships together and we celebrate joys together: at least we are supposed to. The unity God has given us means we can see the difficulties that others in the family face and we can be determined to walk with them rather than just watch them from a distance. Our love is the love of siblings who are utterly committed to one another. Our hearts can be soft, compassionate, and gentle toward one another and we can believe the best of one another, not the worst. So this unity impacts our intentions, our decisions, our responses, our affections, our emotions, and our attitudes.[16]

This way of life takes a determined and clear decision. It demands consistent, intentional attitudes of grace and humility to protect our core convictions around a shared identity, purpose, and destiny. Not only that, but we also need to remind ourselves constantly that protecting the strong ties of unity produces a deep awareness of the whole well-being that God provides to His people, and therefore it is worth the effort.[17]

The world around us has not seen God. They do not know what He looks like or what He sounds like. They have never met Him on the street. That is not their fault. No one has ever seen

God directly like this. When we learn to live in the unity that He has given us, however, those around us see God very clearly in us. They see and experience His love as they see that we love one another. As we make the love and the purpose of God our aim and objective in life, other people see Him in our actions, our attitudes, and our character. The clearest way they see that in our lives is in how we treat one another in the family. When we love one another we are showing that His love is not just a theory but it is also a practical, life-transforming reality in our lives. If God can enable us to love one another with such depth, then He can also help others who have never experienced such love to experience it too. Our togetherness of heart and purpose then becomes a window through which others can see God Himself.[18]

This togetherness can be seen in the way we treat those who are different from us, and it demands a response of humility and grace in us. We should not only spend time with those we like; those who are like us, or those who share our social, political, or cultural outlook. We should not only spend time with those who agree with us! Instead, we need to find ways of putting aside such presumptuous and prideful barriers and self-imposed fences and give our energy to making every possible effort to spend time with those who appear to be somehow less than we are. We need to be careful not to think we are cleverer than others, better than others, wiser than others, or more important than others. An honest and humble understanding of ourselves will help us to relate to others in a much more Christlike way. We need to be careful not to become too big for our boots.[19]

Perhaps we would do well to remember that we are all still learning? Not one of us is a professional or an expert when it comes to believing; instead we are all lifelong students. Unity is strengthened by humility, and humility is easier when we remember that there is only one perfect teacher for us as Christians: His name is Jesus. We are all His followers, first and foremost.[20]

There is good reason for giving Him this central place in our lives and in our commitment to a shared identity, purpose, and destiny. He is the Only One who is able to provide us with a deep sense of connectedness to God and therefore to each other. He is the only one who reconnected us with God and the whole-life peace that God gives us. It was His physical, flesh-and-bone life, His suffering, and His violent death that not only reconnected us with God but also connected us with one another. He Himself removed the enmity, suspicion, and hatred that once locked us into our own narrow points of view and away from other people and their perspectives. He is the Source of our unity together because He is the Source of connection with God and with God's peace.[21]

We have the perfect example to follow, therefore, in our commitment to a shared identity, purpose, and destiny. All the encouragement we need for a deeper commitment to these things is seen in Christ Himself. He provides us with the perfect example of love. By doing so, He inspires us to be like Him in the way we love others. His openness to and dependence upon the Holy Spirit shows us that our commitment to unity is only possible by that same openness and dependence. By looking at the way Jesus thought, lived, and taught we ourselves can become more committed to the kind of togetherness that creates a deep sense of connectedness, understanding, and heartfelt empathy and compassion for others in the Christian family.[22] We stand as siblings in the family of God with our common link being what Jesus Christ has done for us and what He has done in us. As we recognize His centrality and allow our thinking and actions to be shaped by what He has done for us, we are not only clearer about ourselves but we are also able to treat one another as equals in a better way.

When we were baptized we were plunged into Jesus' death and resurrection. In that moment we were stripped of all the previous trappings of how we understood ourselves. Once we have gone through that public rite, stating we belong to Jesus and to His family, we are dressed in Him. That means, in effect, what previously defined us is now irrelevant because He is now the One who defines us. The impact of that is that He not only defines us personally, He also defines how we see one another. Old racial, ethnic, religious, and spiritual dividing lines are destroyed when we become part of Jesus' family. Just as these things are irrelevant, so is our social and economic standing. It doesn't matter whether we are rich or we are poor. It doesn't matter whether someone has more freedom or less freedom than we do. It doesn't even matter any more whether we are male or female. These things have not changed, but the way they define us has! The only thing that matters now is how God defines us. How He defines us shapes how we define ourselves and how we define other people. The basis for those definitions is not what we once were but instead it is what we have become in Jesus Christ. He is both the yardstick of our own lives and the bond that exists between us and the rest of the family.[23]

Our unity flows from Him because He is the Source of our shared identity, purpose, and destiny. Our life flows from Him. Our purpose flows from Him. Our future flows from Him. We are organically and permanently connected to Him because He is the head of our family. That also means that we are organically and permanently connected to all other Christians because we are all part of one body and He is the head of that body. Our connection with Him automatically creates our connection with all other Christians. He is the beating heart at the centre of this body called the church. We are completely and utterly dependent upon His Spirit flowing into us and through us into the family and the wider world. Nothing can change that. The question is whether we are blocking the flow of His Spirit or participating with that flow. Our unity is experienced more deeply when we remember that we are already connected because of what the Father, the Son, and the Holy Spirit have done for us, are doing in us, and will do for us in the future.[24]

So please remember that unity is not something we strive for; it is something we have already been given. It flows from Jesus and what He has done for us. We are His body, organically and permanently connected to Him and therefore intimately, organically, and permanently connected to one another. Every time something happens in God's family in one place, it affects the whole family. We are a single unit, and out of the realization that we are a single unit flows the fuller and deeper experience of our unity. Each of us has a responsibility to find out where we fit in this single unit and then play our part by being connected and committed to Christ and by being connected and committed to one another. If every person who is part of God's family were to behave in this way, there would be no stopping us. We would grow more. We would reach further. We would be more effective. We would love more deeply.[25]

It's worth emphasizing once again that our common identity, common purpose, and common destiny are deeply rooted in what Jesus has already done for us. We are directly connected to Him and to one another in His death and therefore we are directly connected to Him and to one another in our destiny. It is because Jesus has already been resurrected that we have such a common destiny. One day, all of God's people will reign with Him. This is a certainty that is secured by Christ's death and life. Our unity is not something we hope for in the future. It is something already given to us by Jesus that will be displayed more and more fully as time passes. We have a shared future because we share a Saviour.[26]

So let me repeat what I said in the first place. I am pleading with you with all the passion, intensity, and authority that Jesus has given me and because we are each under His Lordship and therefore irrevocably connected to one another. I beg you to recognize that you need to be united and stick together, affirming and acting upon the principle that you should not allow any schisms, divisions, or factions to develop between yourselves. Instead, I urge you to be committed to standing shoulder to shoulder and acting together with a shared and single-minded determination and purpose.[27]

Amen.

Reflection

As you read through this paraphrase of some of the Scriptures that address the issue of unity, think about the implications of the words for your own life and your attitude toward others. Do you give unity the centrality of place that God seems to give it in His word? Have you recognized the deep importance of the spiritual connectedness that

God has established in the relationship between the Father, the Son, and the Holy Spirit and the relationship between both us and God and us and each other?

Why not think about taking this paraphrase and using it as the basis of your prayers for your own church family or for the Christians in your own community over the next month? What would change in you and your ministry if protecting and promoting unity were to be given this kind of emphasis?

Confessing Our Division

There can be little doubt that the church of Jesus Christ has failed spectacularly to live out this shared identity and to grasp its full significance for us. As a result of this failure our shared sense of hope, mission, and calling are jeopardized. If you were not a Christian and you were observing the church at either a local or a national level, it would be easy to believe that what divides us is more important than what unites us.

Take just two aspects of the church's life as an example of this mistake, namely Holy Communion and baptism. These two rites within the life of the church are two of the most obvious moments in the life of an individual Christian where we identify with the wider body of the Lord Jesus Christ. When we participate in Holy Communion, we mark the death of Christ on the cross and the reality that through His death all Christians gain access to forgiveness, life, hope, healing, and a relationship with God. When we are baptized, we are displaying our membership of Christ and of His body, the church, for the whole world to see. These two rites are among the most obvious expressions of unity that we have as Christians, yet they are probably two of the most divisive issues in the relationships between many churches. A great deal of ink has been consumed in expressing differing views on the meanings and modes of both baptism and Holy Communion. What is more worrying is that blood has also been spilled over the issues. I will comment on baptism later in the book, but how do we approach Holy Communion without dividing?

Even as I write these words I face a conundrum. How do I describe Holy Communion in a way that will not offend someone? Is it best to talk about the Lord's Table or would it be better to talk about the Eucharist? Perhaps I should think about the Breaking of Bread, or do I need to talk about Mass? Will I offend people if I use terms for this rite that display my personal convictions around the bread and wine being symbols only rather than being or becoming the actual body and blood of the Lord Jesus Christ? Should I talk about Holy Communion being an act of remembrance? If I refer to Holy Communion as one of the two sacraments of the church, what will those who believe in other sacraments think, and what will those who see all of life as sacramental and reject the notion of any specific sacraments think?

I do not need to illustrate the point any further. The sensitivity around Holy Communion is just one example of the fragility of the ways in which we often think or talk about unity in the church.

Weaknesses in unity

It seems to me that we have often failed to bear witness to the unity of our faith, the unity of our mission, and the unity of our family. This failure is not only conceptual; it is also visible. It is seen in the local church that is riven by suspicion and resentment of one another and in leadership teams that fail to lay down their own agendas for the greater good of the kingdom of God. Division and lack of unity is seen in the unhealthy comparisons, duplication, and one-upmanship across churches in a local community when there is fear of the success of another church and a defensive claim of ownership upon the lives of individual believers by one church when those believers choose, perhaps for very good reasons, to move their congregational allegiance to another local church.

The terrible impact of division is also seen nationally when denominations have very public fights over what they believe and how they live out their faith. One of the great challenges of our divided witness is that the world around us looks at the church and scratches its head in incredulity over the way we behave toward one another and the things that we can say. Witnessing our vitriol toward one another is a painful thing. If you have any doubt about that then simply spend an hour or so listening to a Christian who has been hurt by other believers.

As mentioned earlier, watching the way Christians talk to one another on the internet in general and on social media in particular is perhaps the most obvious example of how hurtful we can be. As a Christian, I sometimes feel thoroughly ashamed of the way we treat one another. We can choose our friends, but we cannot choose our family. Our belittling of a brother or sister in Christ, our dismissal of their point of view, or our public castigation of them without any sense of love or grace does not change God's view of them for a moment. If they are in His family then they are in our family. I remember reading somewhere once that if God chooses to call someone a son or a daughter then we dare not ever treat them as anything other than a brother or a sister.

Of course, there will be times when we engage in a public exchange of ideas where we strongly disagree with one another. Such situations are not always bad, and they are not always wrong. If a statement is made publicly and you disagree with it, then in many senses it must be addressed publicly. Paul did this in addressing false teaching, and so can we. The important thing is to ensure that we maintain grace, love, and kindness in how we speak to one another and about one another.

Avoiding schism and division

If we treat our family badly, then how on earth do we expect people to join it? Surely those whom we are seeking to win into the family of God would be put off by behaviour that makes that family look fractured, angry, and judgmental? Brothers and sisters, the world is watching us and how we behave. Often others are unable to hear what we are saying because of the noise of who we are. When Paul wrote to the Corinthian church he reminded them that they were living epistles, being read by all (2 Corinthians 3:2). Our convictions and our conduct need to match. The old adage is very true: people will not care how much we know until they know how much we care, and they will gauge how much we might care for them by how much we care for one another.

We must be careful to avoid schism if at all possible, instead doing everything we can to maintain the unity of the Spirit in the bond of peace (Ephesians 4:3). The very fact that there are so many denominations and streams within the church of Jesus Christ is evidence enough of our ability to separate rather than to stick together. Perhaps it is our strong belief in the invisible church at the expense of any notion of an institutional church that causes us to skip over the terrible sore of our endless proliferation. We are, in that regard, more like Lloyd-Jones than we are Stott. Or maybe we have become too comfortable within our own stream. We simply find it harder to see the beauty of other expressions of Christian community. Or perhaps we ourselves are indoctrinated with our own sense of rightness at the expense of others? Or maybe, just maybe, the importance of unity is simply lost on us? We don't think it matters that much. Perhaps we see the issue of Christian disunity as a ball of knots that cannot be untied? Whatever the reasons for not addressing the issue of unity, there are stronger reasons for addressing it. I will look at some of the theological arguments for working together later, but for now let me highlight just four pragmatic reasons for strengthening our unity.

1. We are stronger together

We have more resources when we work together. We have better coverage when we work together. We are more coherent when we work together. We are more humble when we work together. We are more beautiful when we work together. We are more attractive to others when we work together. We are more faithful to God when we work together. The purposes and plans of God are more effectively accomplished and fulfilled when we as the church, the people who claim to belong to God on earth, stand together and serve together. We are stronger together, and therefore the opposite is also true: we are weaker apart. A united church is a stronger church.

As we seek to engage with society we are much more effective when we stand together and speak collectively. I have been passionate about the church's witness in the world for many years. At one point my role was the head of mission, evangelism, and prayer for the Evangelical Alliance. A little later I led a charity called Faithworks which sought to help local churches to get involved with their local communities without compromising their

Christian convictions. I continue to act as a champion of the role of local churches in their communities and the role of the church in society by advising a number of charities and churches as well as working with various aspects of government locally, nationally, and internationally. In each and every case where churches work together for the good of their community their impact is stronger.

Cinnamon Network began to emerge in 2010 in response to growing social need, public sector reform, increasing recognition of the role of voluntary organizations, and the economic cuts. Fifty Christian CEOs and leaders were challenged to consider how the Christian community could deliver more local transformation on a national scale, and do so at speed. They met together at The Cinnamon Club in London and Cinnamon Network was born. Their aim is to serve the nation, and they do this by enabling people and sharing resources to help Christians to be part of the transformation of local communities and to help those in social need. The Network does this by championing church-based social action, building partnerships between churches and civic groups, and delivering actionable research that enables effective support by churches to local communities. Cinnamon Network received an award from the Prime Minister in June 2013, who said:

> *By supporting churches to address the most pressing issues in their neighbourhoods The Cinnamon Network is transforming communities for the better. The award reflects the outstanding work done by both the recognised projects and people in local churches who willingly give up their time on the front line.*[28]

Gather is a national network of vibrant missional unity movements across the United Kingdom.[29] It also links to other similar movements around the world. All over the country in cities, towns, and villages, God has been doing a hidden work. Christian leaders and churches over the last few years have been forming vibrant mission-focused unity movements based on a foundation of prayer and friendship. Hundreds of these groups exist, providing examples of extraordinary partnerships and what can happen when churches work together. These are people who are fed up with working in isolation from, or in competition with, other churches in their area. They are laying down secondary theological and cultural differences for the sake of reaching their local area with the love of Christ.

Both Cinnamon Network and Gather demonstrate the reality that when local churches put aside their differences and work together, they reach more people, speak more clearly, and have a greater impact.

In 2007 I wrote a book called *Kingdom Come: The Local Church as a Catalyst for Social Change* in which I outlined the call and the opportunities of local churches working together. One of the things I said in that book was this:

> *Followers of Christ, whatever our theological differences and preferences, are each part of His Church and we have been given the privilege and power to live as people of this kingdom [of God], demonstrating its power and purpose in our lives, in our communities and indeed throughout the world. The kingdom of God is not labelled with terms such as evangelical or liberal. We must not alienate our brothers and sisters in our efforts to be servants of God. How can we proclaim a message of the kingdom to our communities if we do not also acknowledge our love of those within the family of God and*

our devotion to one another? Every Christian in the world, and every local church is called to an orientation around this one simple reality – "Jesus is Lord"; and to demonstrate His lordship in our personal lives, in our commitments to one another and in our service of the world.[30]

It is as clear as day to me: we are stronger together and we are weaker apart. This has been the settled commitment of my heart for thirty years. It has shaped my ministry. I pray it will do so for the rest of my life.

2. We need one another

In the local community that I am part of we are privileged to enjoy a high degree of unity across the local churches. We share ideas, programmes, mission outreaches, prayer times, and resources. Our young adults meet across the churches regularly, as do our youth workers, worship leaders, and pastors. This sense of common purpose can sometimes be a bit frustrating because it brings with it challenges of different church cultures, leadership styles, and decision-making processes, but it also brings with it life, diversity, and joy. The reality is that we need one another. None of us has the capacity to reach the whole community on our own.

In 2012 we ran an Olympic Outreach together as local churches called "Run the Race". It was a mammoth task that involved hundreds of volunteers to reach thousands of people. I remember it well because it was during the three-week period of the outreach that my mum became a Christian. The team was led by one of my colleagues, Martyn Groves, and someone from each of the other churches. It was a rip-roaring success. To see thousands of people flock to events, and the two communities of Chalfont St Peter and Gerrards Cross buzzing with what was happening, was an amazing experience. Best of all, when locals asked us who was making it all happen, we were able to say with great joy that it was the church.

None of our congregations could have achieved what we did on our own. We needed one another in so many ways. The mission is a simple reminder to me that God has designed us to be a body together as the church. We simply cannot do what He has called us to do on our own.

3. Denominationalism is on the wane

Denominationalism is becoming less significant. There are many who welcome that change. If the truth be told, those coming after us care less about our divisions and more about our actions.

There are not many people who are part of Gold Hill, the church that I have the joy of leading, simply because we are a Baptist church. The vast majority of people who have made Gold Hill their church family have done so because they feel connected to God and connected to one another as part of this believing community, and their hearts chime with the overarching missional focus and direction of the church. They feel at home with our style of worship and the tenor and style of our preaching. Our core statement of faith makes sense to them. Of course, they have a sense of being equipped for life and service of Christ and they believe that they are taught the truth about God and His purposes in the world. Additionally, they have a sense of being pastored, supported, and loved. Being part of this local church gives them a sense of accountability and an opportunity to break bread with other believers of like mind and heart. The style and personality of our church family seem to fit for them. They also choose to be part of our church family because they have a sense of connection with our overarching vision and values. The majority of our church family, however, are not deeply driven by denominational affiliation. There are a few who have made their home with us because they attended another Baptist church somewhere else before coming to live in our area, but not many.

It seems to me that denominationalism itself seems to be less important to many people today. There are people who are part of Gold Hill who are from a Pentecostal background, others from the Brethren, some from the Roman Catholic tradition, still others from an Anglican heritage, and those who come to us from the Methodist family. You would be hard pressed to look out at our congregation and guess who was from where. Whether they come from no church background at all or from one of the many streams and tribes of church life that exist in the world, they are less concerned about such secondary labels and more concerned about being faithful to God in the world and reaching others with the good news of Jesus Christ.

Not everything about denominationalism is wrong, as we will explore in a later chapter, but as denominational boundaries become less clear and affiliations become less important, it is perhaps time for us to acknowledge that we are entering a new season in the life of the church around the world. That new season may address some of the unhelpful tendencies of schism, division, and separation that denominationalism has brought with it over the years.

4. We have more resilience together

I am not sure that those who say that the United Kingdom is becoming more resistant to the gospel are right. I have discovered an increasing openness to hearing the good news of Jesus over recent years and I am hugely optimistic about the future of the church in this nation. I think the same is true for the other countries that I have visited, including the United States of America. What I think is true, however, is that where Christian faith is opposed, those who oppose it are becoming more resistant and more determined to undermine the church.

Simultaneously we are facing a new interest in the gospel by many and a strengthened opposition to the church by some. The challenge is that often those who oppose the church have positions of influence and power in our society. In his book, *God's Unwelcome Recovery*, Sean Oliver-Dee persuasively suggests that the "new establishment" in Britain is seeking to paint a picture in Britain of a church that is in terminal decline for three reasons. Firstly, they don't want to talk about religion; secondly, they believe that the death of religion is good for society; thirdly, religion gets in the way of a continually improving world and belongs to a worldview that should be banished.[31]

What is this new establishment?

As Simon Kuper describes in his article for the "Financial Times", the new establishment is an elite that has developed outside of old class structures (although it still owes much to an Oxbridge education). It is an elite based on intellectual ability and an adherence to certain common perceptions, centred around London, that you can become a member of

if, as Kuper describes, "you are clever and behave yourself."…
they are vehemently opposed to the manifestation of any kind
of religion.[32]

In this dichotomy of a readiness to explore faith on the one hand among many people and an increased resistance to the gospel by some, a united church is going to be much more able to support one another. We have more resilience together than we do on our own. There is an old African proverb which states, "Where there is no enemy within, the enemies outside cannot hurt you." The phrase was reportedly used by Winston Churchill on more than one occasion during the Second World War to remind the British people of the need to stand together.

Whatever the level of resistance or opposition the church might face in the United Kingdom and in other parts of the world, we are undoubtedly able to handle it more effectively as we support one another. One of my predecessors at Gold Hill, the late Jim Graham, would often remind the congregation that there was enough discouragement and criticism of the church outside the community of faith for us to cope with without us adding to the burden by being divided inside the church.

Conclusion

There are so many pragmatic reasons for working together and for strengthening unity across churches that it is impossible to list them all. Highlighting just four seems so inadequate. One could add such things as the economy of scale, the increased effectiveness in advocacy, the improvement of communication when local churches have a single spokesperson, the ability that partnership brings in enabling specific local churches to specialize in the ministries they provide, the greater likelihood of reaching a broader socio-political demographic, the ways in which partnership lifts the pressure on churches to feel as if they have to have all the answers all the time. All of these and many other reasons for working together are good arguments for increased unity. The four that I have detailed in a greater way here are simply examples.

As I noted earlier, however, there are more than simply pragmatic reasons for working together and increasing unity; there are deeply biblical ones too. It is to these that I turn now, but as I prepare to do so, I am reminded of something I wrote in the first book I ever published:

> It is my deep conviction that a movement of people committed to social justice and societal transformation can make things better...
>
> I want to join you in building a better world and I am convinced that if we can only work together we will achieve so much more than we would if we worked apart. My longing is that together we can discover the spiritual energy and passion that will keep us going and help us to see beyond the pain we encounter so often in our own lives and in the lives of others.
>
> However deep the struggle, however long the road, there is hope. I am convinced that God is at work in the world through those who are committed to making a difference for the better. The world will be a better place – and your work is helping it become one.[33]

Reflection

If it is true that we are stronger together, that we need one another, that denominationalism is dying, and that we have greater resilience together, what are the implications of these principles on how your ministry is fulfilled and your church is led? Have you been guilty of treating people in your local church as if they were the property of the local church? Have you criticized those who have left while welcoming those who join your church from a different one? How can you avoid creating a culture where you behave as if your church is better than all the others in the area? How can you deliberately speak well of other churches?

Take some time to think about the good things that you can see in the other churches in your community. Perhaps you could write a letter of thanks to their leaders, or a letter of apology if it is needed. Does your church have resources that you could share with others? Those resources could include money, facilities, people, or experience. Are there local mission networks or leaders' groups that you could get involved with? Perhaps you could think about projects in your community that you could start or become part of?

Are there people in your church who would benefit from encouragement and relationship with people in other churches who do the same job as they do? How might you link the Christian teachers in your community, or the Christian managers or directors? How can you take a more joined-up approach to the ministry of Christians in the workplace and in the local community?

Lastly, what could you do nationally to stand with other Christians? Perhaps your church could join the Evangelical Alliance, or you could encourage those who are part of your church to do so. Maybe you could get behind a national Christian aid agency such as

Samaritan's Purse or Tearfund or World Vision. Could your church family support the persecuted church through Open Doors or through Christian Solidarity Worldwide? Think of creative ways in which you can tell the story of the wider church to those in your own local church.

Christ's Cry for His People –
That We May Be One

"I ask not only on behalf of these, but also on behalf of those who will believe in me through their word, that they may all be one. As you, Father, are in me and I am in you, may they also be in us, so that the world may believe that you have sent me. The glory that you have given me I have given them, so that they may be one, as we are one, I in them and you in me, that they may become completely one, so that the world may know that you have sent me and have loved them even as you have loved me. Father, I desire that those also, whom you have given me, may be with me where I am, to see my glory, which you have given me because you loved me before the foundation of the world.

"Righteous Father, the world does not know you, but I know you; and these know that you have sent me. I made your name known to them, and I will make it known, so that the love with which you have loved me may be in them, and I in them."

John 17:20–26

On the night that He was arrested, Jesus prayed that we would be one. In one of the most difficult moments of His entire ministry, with the cross looming before Him and guards on the way to arrest Him, He asked His Father that we would be one. The fact that He prayed this prayer at this particular moment in His life brings a hush to the soul:

> *No attempt to describe the prayer can give a just idea of its sublimity, its pathos, its touching yet exalted character, its tone at once of tenderness and triumphant expectation.*[34]

His prayer appears in John 17, and it is the longest prayer of Jesus we have recorded. There can be few things more challenging to us as Christians than reading these words slowly, prayerfully, and thoughtfully and then asking ourselves whether we are living in such a way that we could say we are part of the answer to this cry from the Saviour or not. In the words of Tom Wright:

> *When you make this prayer your own, when you enter into this chapter and see what happens, you are being invited to come into the heart of that intimate relation between Jesus and the Father and have it, so to speak, happen all around you. This is both what the prayer embodies and also its central subject matter.*[35]

What did Jesus actually pray?

John 17 is sometimes called the high priestly prayer of Jesus,[36] although not all would agree with this description.[37] As we read through the prayer itself, we hear echoes of the principles and priorities of the Lord's Prayer (Matthew 6:9–13; Luke 11:2–4), that God would be glorified, that His will would be done, that His people would be protected from evil and kept Holy, and that His kingdom would be established fully. Whatever we call it, the prayer of Jesus detailed to us in John 17 sits at the heart of any understanding of what it means to be united as His people. Underlying the whole prayer is Jesus' deep desire that His Father's will be done in His own life, in the lives of those who are following Him, and in the lives of those who will follow Him.

There are a variety of ways of breaking down the prayer, but for my purposes I suggest that a simple of understanding of its structure is as follows:

1. In verses 1–5 Jesus prays for Himself and His glorification.

2. In verses 6–19 Jesus prays for the circle of His immediate disciples.

3. In verses 20–23 Jesus prays for those who will believe in Him from that moment onwards.

4. In verses 24–26 Jesus prays for all those who believe to be perfected and to see His glory.

I want to focus on the second half of the prayer of Jesus recorded in John 17, the part of the prayer in which He prays for those who will believe in Him from that moment onward. To do that, however, it is important to take a few moments to set that half of the prayer in context, because it is always dangerous to isolate a passage of Scripture from its context.

John places the prayer within what is commonly called the Farewell Discourse, sometimes called the Last Supper Discourse, which is found between John 14 and John 17 inclusively. The meal is referred to in Matthew 26, Mark 14, and Luke 22, but John does not mention it. Instead he focuses on Jesus washing the feet of His disciples as recorded in John 13. John 18 tells us what Jesus did after He had finished praying:

After Jesus had spoken these words, he went out with his disciples across the Kidron valley to a place where there was a garden, which he and his disciples entered.

John 18:1

Themes of the prayer

John's record of the prayer itself picks up many of the themes of the rest of his Gospel. He is very interested in the idea of Jesus' glory being revealed and the hour at which this will happen. He speaks of the idea of glory in his prologue, and he speaks of these two ideas of glory and Jesus' hour in the first sign that he records, when Jesus turns water into wine as well as at the beginning of the prayer:

And the word became flesh and lived among us, and we have seen his glory, the glory as of a father's only son, full of grace and truth.

John 1:14

And Jesus said to her, "Woman, what concern is that to you and to me? My hour has not yet come."

John 2:4

Jesus did this, the first of his signs, in Cana in Galilee, and revealed his glory; and his disciples believed in him.

John 2:11

"Father, the hour has come; glorify your Son so that the Son may glorify you."

John 17:1

John also picks up ideas of truth and life in the prayer to which he first alludes at the very beginning of his Gospel, as well as at the very end; he also refers to these ideas at other points, for example:

> *All things came into being through him, and without him not one thing came into being. What has come into being in him was life, and the life was the light of all people. The light shines in the darkness, and the darkness did not overcome it.*
>
> John 1:3–5

> *Now Jesus did many other signs in the presence of his disciples, which are not written in this book. But these are written so that you may come to believe that Jesus is the Messiah, the Son of God, and that through believing you may have life in his name.*
>
> John 20:30–31

> *"The thief comes only to steal and kill and destroy. I came that they may have life, and have it abundantly."*
>
> John 10:10

> *"I am the good shepherd. I know my own and my own know me, just as the Father knows me and I know the Father. And I lay down my life for the sheep."*
>
> John 10:14–15

> *Jesus said to him, "I am the way, and the truth, and the life. No one comes to the Father except through me."*
>
> John 14:6

> *"And this is eternal life, that they may know you, the only true God, and Jesus Christ, whom you have sent."*
>
> John 17:3

We also have the idea of the Father and the Son working together, which is an image repeated across John's Gospel (for example, see John 5:17; 6:29). And John picks up the idea of the disciples being separate from the world in Jesus' prayer. John's use of the image of the world is at one moment used to show how much God loves it and at another used to show how much God opposes the systems and structures of the world:

> He was in the world, and the world came into being through him; yet the world did not know him.
>
> John 1:10

> "For God so loved the world that he gave his only Son, so that everyone who believes in him may not perish but may have eternal life."
>
> John 3:16

> "If the world hates you, be aware that it hated me before it hated you. If you belonged to the world, the world would love you as its own. Because you do not belong to the world, but I have chosen you out of the world – therefore the world hates you."
>
> John 15:18–19

> "I have given them your word, and the world has hated them because they do not belong to the world, just as I do not belong to the world. I am not asking you to take them out of the world, but I ask you to protect them from the evil one. They do not belong to the world, just as I do not belong to the world. Sanctify them in the truth; your word is truth. As you have sent me into the world, so I have sent them into the word.

And for their sakes I sanctify myself, so that they also may be sanctified in truth."

John 17:14–19

"My kingdom is not from this world. If my kingdom were from this world, my followers would be fighting to keep me from being handed over to the Jews. But as it is, my kingdom is not from here."

John 18:36

Finally, the idea of where Jesus abides is repeated in the prayer and picks up a similar theme across the Gospel:

They said to him, "Rabbi" (which translated means Teacher), "where are you staying?"

John 1:38

"Rabbi, we know that you are a teacher who has come from God; for no one can do these signs that you do apart from the presence of God."

John 3:2

"If you keep my commandments, you will abide in my love, just as I have kept my Father's commandments and abide in his love."

John 15:10

"So now, Father, glorify me in your own presence, with the glory that I had in your presence before the world existed… Now they know that everything you have given me is from you; for the words that you gave to me I have given to them,

and they have received them and know in truth that I came
from you; and they have believed that you sent me."

John 17:5, 7–8

So as we approach the prayer of Jesus we have the sense that this prayer is linked to God's glory as displayed in and through the Lord Jesus Christ at the appointed time; that somehow Jesus is praying for His disciples to be protected in the world, that they will continue to abide in Him as He abides in His Father; and that in Jesus there is light, life, hope, and truth. All of these threads weave their way into His prayer for His disciples which is, as I have already said, rooted in the Father's purpose and glory.

The requests of Jesus

Reading through the prayer, we discover that there are seven specific requests. Firstly, Jesus twice asks the Father to glorify the Son:

"Father, the hour has come; glorify your Son so that the Son
may glorify you."

John 17:1

"So now, Father, glorify me in your own presence with the
glory that I had in your presence before the world existed."

John 17:5

Next Jesus prays for the men and women who are His immediate disciples, asking His Father to protect them in the world as well as from the devil or from evil (depending on which original manuscript your translation is based on), and to sanctify them in the truth:

"Holy Father, protect them in your name that you have given me, so that they may be one, as we are one."

John 17:11

"I am not asking you to take them out of the world, but I ask you to protect them from the evil one [or from evil]."

John 17:15

"Sanctify them in the truth; your word is truth."

John 17:17

Lastly, Jesus prays for those who will believe in Him through the witness of His immediate disciples and on into the future. He prays that they will be one in a way that reflects His own relationship with His Father and His Father's relationship with Him, and so that the world will believe that the Father did indeed send His Son. Jesus also prays that those who have been given to Him will be with Him and see His glory:

"I ask not only on behalf of these, but also on behalf of those who will believe in me through their word, that they may all be one. As you, Father, are in me and I am in you, may they also be in us, so that the world may believe that you have sent me."

John 17:20–21

"Father, I desire that those also, whom you have given me, may be with me where I am, to see my glory."

John 17:24

What does Jesus mean when He prays that we will be one in verses 20–23?

Taking all of those specific requests into consideration, it is clear that Jesus prays for His Father to be glorified; for His immediate disciples to be protected, sanctified, and held through and in the truth; and for all who will believe in Him to be held together and kept as one "through their word" (John 17:20–21). There are profound implications from all of this for how we understand the nature of Jesus' prayer and the way in which we go about unity.[38]

Having cleared the decks somewhat, let's take a look at each portion of the second part of Jesus' prayer to see if we can understand it more clearly.

1. The parameters of our unity – every believer

"I ask not only on behalf of these, but also on behalf of those who will believe in me through their word, that they may all be one."

John 17:20–21

It is patently obvious that in John 17:20–21, Jesus prays that the Father would make His people one, but we must not turn that prayer into a blanket approval of ecumenism and togetherness. The prayer of Jesus is deeply rooted in ideas of truth, sanctification, and God's ultimate purposes. Unity for unity's sake does not sit at the heart of this prayer. Instead, we see something different emerge.

As Jesus turns His attention to those who will believe in Him from the moment of His prayer onwards, we read these words:

"I ask not only on behalf of these, but also on behalf of those who will believe in me through their word…"

John 17:20

It seems clear to me that Jesus is linking His prayer for all those believers who will come after Him with His prayer for those who are His disciples at this moment in His earthly ministry. And what is the link between us and them? We are linked to them "through their word". He has prayed three times about the Father's word as He has prayed for His immediate disciples:

"They have kept your word."

John 17:6

"I have given them your word."

John 17:14

"Sanctify them in the truth; your word is truth."

John 17:17

Now, however, He talks of "their" word, as He prays for us:

"I ask not only on behalf of these, but also on behalf of those who will believe in me through their word, that they may all be one."

John 17:20–21

All that Jesus prays for us is linked to what He has prayed for his contemporaneous disciples, and all that He prays for His contemporaneous disciples is linked to what He prays for Himself. This means that His prayer that we "all may be one" (John 17:21) is intricately bound up with faithfulness to the words of His followers, with holiness that flows from His words and theirs at work in us, with being distinctive in the world and committed to holiness, with being protected from the work of evil in general and from the evil one in particular, and with placing the hour of Christ's glorification, namely His cross, at the centre of our own lives. J. C. Ryle puts the sentiment behind the prayer of Jesus in John 17:20 this way:

> *"I now pray also for all who shall believe on Me through the preaching of my disciples in all future time, and not for my eleven apostles only."*[39]

The words of Jesus' prayer in John 17:20 are a radical and powerful cry to His Father for a unity that is tightly bound to His purposes, His power, and His plan. Too often, these words are used to justify an approach to unity that dismisses truth and disregards the call of Christ upon His people to faithful life and witness. As a result, unity itself becomes bland and lifeless. If we are not careful, our quest for unity becomes a quest in and of itself. We must be careful not to strip this prayer for unity of its power:

> *This is not simply a "unity of love". It is a unity predicated on adherence to the revelation the Father mediated to the first disciples through his Son, the revelation they accepted… and then passed on.*[40]

The unity Christ longs for is one which is deeply rooted in the truth and therefore rooted in Him. The more we allow ourselves to be more like Christ, the closer we will come to other Christians. We do not build unity by pretending there are no differences among us. We build unity by pursuing the Christ who has pursued us. Perhaps the great challenge is that we often seek unity by comparing and contrasting our convictions with one another, instead of allowing our unity to flow from our mutual convictions which are rooted in God Himself.

The American pastor and writer, A. W. Tozer (1901–63), wrote:

> *Has it ever occurred to you that one hundred pianos all tuned to the same fork are automatically tuned to each other? They are of one accord by being tuned, not to each other, but to another standard to which each one must individually bow. So one hundred worshipers met together, each one looking away to Christ, are in heart nearer to each other than they could possibly be, were they to become "unity" conscious and turn their eyes away from God to strive for closer fellowship. Social religion is perfected when private religion is purified. The body becomes stronger as its members become healthier. The whole Church of God gains when the members that compose it begin to seek a better and a higher life.*[41]

All those who are Christians are loved by the same Father, redeemed by the same Saviour, and empowered by the same Spirit. We are all Jesus Christ's followers, and God has given us the same instructions. He has placed us in one story, the Great Story of His purposes on the earth. As Christ's family we all trace our spiritual ancestry back to the same set of events over the period of thirty-three or thirty-four years between around 4 BC and AD 30 that revolved around His birth, His life, His death, His resurrection, His Ascension, Him pouring out His Spirit on His people, and His promise to return to the earth. Our lives are about God's purposes, and some of God's purposes revolve around unity. As controversial as it might sound, I do wonder whether we spend too much time trying to agree with one another and not enough time asking God to make us more like Him.

The prayer of Jesus is for all those who will follow Him and believe in Him. The kind of unity that John has in mind with the phrase "those who will believe in me through their word" (John 17:20) embeds this idea of unity in the convictions of the word and of faith. As we will see in a moment, this is not an easy unity. It is not a superficial and light unity. It has as its basis the Father and the Son. It is not founded on some misplaced concept of institutional ecclesiology, nor is it based on purely historical data. It cannot be man-made or manufactured by forced organizational structures. At best, such structures can only point to the real unity that Christ prays for, and at worst they can give the thin veneer of unity on the surface with nothing substantial beneath. The breathtaking reality is that wherever the true gospel is proclaimed, a powerful, organic, and transformative unity exists that points all the way back to the prayer of Christ, which is continually answered when we are faithful to Him and to His purposes. When we waiver from His purposes, that unity is not broken. And therein lies one of the great challenges with which we must grapple.

2. The pain of our unity

The idea that the unity for which Jesus prays in John 17 involves us avoiding hard conversations or difficult decisions around our beliefs, our mission, and our behaviours just does not fit with the wider context of the whole passage. Christian unity is not the art of avoiding the difficult issues. Unity is not the same as keeping the peace. I have discovered that often what is described as unity is really nothing more than a list of beliefs and behaviours that everyone can live with. Controversial issues, hot topics, and contested areas of theological conviction are off limits. That kind of unity is fatally flawed. I think the unity that Jesus prays for in John 17 is a unity that expresses itself in a love for brothers and sisters *no matter what.*

Perhaps Augustine's approach to the Donatists in Carthage was right after all, that even when we have sharp disagreements we must learn to love one another, to find a way through. What would happen if we were to make the simple decision that we would refuse to walk away from the table? I do not mean that we give up on the truth, rather I mean quite the opposite. What if our unity were to express itself in a fundamental commitment that we would not take the easy route of turning our back on a brother or sister, even when we had a fundamental disagreement with them? That would make unity so much harder, but it might also make it much more meaningful.

Hard choices and difficult conversations

Paul argues in 1 Corinthians 8 that Christians must learn to give up their freedoms for the sake of other Christians. There was clearly a disagreement between the believers Corinth about whether Christians should be eating meat that had been previously offered as sacrifices in the pagan temples. Paul roots the conversation firmly in the principles of our unity in God, in precisely the same way as Jesus roots His prayer in John 17, reminding the Corinthians that there is only one true God and that all who love Him are known by Him (1 Corinthians 8:3). He argues that those who find it difficult to eat meat offered to idols have a weaker conscience (1 Corinthians 8:7–8). He then goes on to urge them not to allow this issue to become one over which they divide:

> But take care that this liberty of yours does not somehow become a stumbling block to the weak. For if others see you, who possess knowledge, eating in the temple of an idol, might they not, since their conscience is weak, be encouraged to the point of eating food sacrificed to idols? So by your knowledge those weak believers for whom Christ died are destroyed. But when you thus sin against members of your family, and wound their conscience when it is weak, you sin against Christ. Therefore, if food is a cause of their falling, I will never eat meat, so that I may not cause one of them to fall.
>
> 1 Corinthians 8:9–13

Paul follows a similar argument in Romans 14. He begins by addressing the very same issue of eating meat offered to idols (Romans 14:1–4). He then takes the example of giving honour to one day above others (Romans 14:5–6). After using the two examples, Paul focuses in on the issues that sit behind them both. Christians are not free to do what we want, believe what we want, or live as we want because we no longer belong to ourselves alone:

> We do not live to ourselves, and we do not die to ourselves. If we live, we live to the Lord, and if we die, we die to the Lord; so then, whether we live or whether we die, we are the Lord's. For to this end Christ died and lived again, so that he might be Lord of both the living and the dead.
>
> Romans 14:7–10

He reminds the Roman Christians that each of us is accountable to God for our actions and our choices (Romans 14:12). He urges them to think differently about their disagreements, which are of a secondary nature:

> *Let us therefore no longer pass judgement on one another, but resolve instead never to put a stumbling-block or hindrance in the way of another. I know and am persuaded in the Lord Jesus that nothing is unclean in itself; but it is unclean for anyone who thinks it unclean. If your brother or sister is being injured by what you eat, you are no longer walking in love. Do not let what you eat cause the ruin of one for whom Christ died. So do not let your good be spoken of as evil. For the kingdom of God is not food and drink but righteousness and peace and joy in the Holy Spirit. The one who thus serves Christ is acceptable to God and has human approval. Let us then pursue what makes for peace and for mutual edification. Do not, for the sake of food, destroy the work of God. Everything is indeed clean, but it is wrong for you to make others fall by what you eat; it is good not to eat meat or drink wine or do anything that makes your brother or sister stumble. The faith that you have, have as your own conviction before God. Blessed are those who have no reason to condemn themselves because of what they approve. But those who have doubts are condemned if they eat, because they do not act from faith; for whatever does not proceed from faith is sin.*
>
> Romans 14:13–23

The implications are clear. Our actions and our choices should reflect our fundamental commitment to one another in Christ. Paul is not suggesting here that issues are avoided or that subjects are not discussed. Instead he is describing a robust unity that is rooted in who Christ is and what He has done.

Interestingly, in both cases Paul's argument is countercultural to the way we would look at it. He suggests that those who do not eat meat or who honour a particular day are the weaker brothers or sisters in terms of their understanding, and that the stronger brother or sister is the one who holds a strong view on the issue. He then goes on to argue, however, that the stronger brother or sister should abstain from the behaviour that they consider acceptable for the sake of the weaker brother or sister. He does not suggest for a single moment that the issue doesn't matter, and the text leaves no hint of the issue being swept under the carpet. Instead, he reminds them of their unity in Christ which should determine their actions and attitudes to one another.

There are so many differences of opinion among Christians that we could never list them all. Some, like the eating of meat or the observance of a special day, are secondary issues that do not affect our salvation. Others, such as belief in grace or the power of the cross or the importance of faith, are primary issues. Failure to hold to a primary issue would mean that a person is not, in fact, a follower of Jesus Christ at all. Difference of opinion on a secondary issue does not mean someone is not a Christian; it simply means they have a different view.

Then there are those issues that some would see as secondary and some would see as primary. These are the tricky ones. They are the ones that lead churches to split and tempers to rise. Is baptism a primary or a secondary issue? Where would we place our views on Holy Communion? Do the roles and responsibilities of church government fall into a primary category or a secondary one? What about the ways in which we read and interpret the Bible? Would we say that the issue of the tradition and role of the church is a primary or a secondary issue for unity? What about the role of women? What do we do about the issue of divorce? Do the different views around human sexuality and gender fall into the category of primary importance or the category of secondary importance?

These are the sorts of questions that divide the church. One person's primary issue is another person's secondary issue. How we handle them determines whether we stay together or turn and go in our separate directions. There is, however, a way forward. We do not need to become clones of one another and all behave in exactly the same way. The key to a unity that works is remembering that unity itself is not the goal.

3. The principle of our unity – love modelled in the Godhead

"As you, Father, are in me and I am in you, may they also be in us… I in them and you in me, that they may be completely one."
John 17:21, 23

The unity described here and for which Christ prays is a deep, intimate affair. It does not reflect a willingness to agree to disagree, but instead reflects a profound sense of mutual affection, shared identity, and common understanding. So much is this the case that Jesus describes the unity He prays for as being reflective of the unity that exists between the Father and the Son. There is no division of understanding here, nor is there a division of intention.

They have perfect love, perfect complementarity, perfect understanding, and perfect union. Their unity is not only skin deep. It is a unity of purpose that will be tested in the upcoming furnace of the cross. There are no fissures or cracks in it. It will stand the test of time. It is rooted in truth, goodness, and hope. It has no questions, no hidden agendas, and no controlling desires. It is permanent, perfect, and powerful. This is the unity that Christ prays His Father will give His people. Compare this beautiful ideal to the way in which we often seek to achieve unity.

When we seek unity we do things to try to discourage disunity, and that ends up destroying the very conditions that foster unity in the first place. If we make unity the goal we might end up being pleasant to one another on the surface, but under the surface we have damaged our foundations. If we recognize that true unity flows first from being rooted in Christ, we then begin to find a way forward, however hard it might be. The tuning fork is set to Christ, not to the issue or to the position of the other person. True biblical unity requires openness, honesty, and a willingness to address the hard questions. Unity for unity's sake sacrifices openness and honesty for fear of causing offence. To be truly united we seek to love as Christ loved, to listen as Christ listened, and to live as Christ lived. Love forgives when we are wronged. Love shrugs off differences of opinion. Love isn't afraid to say the hard thing. Love seeks the well-being of the other person, not just the defence of our own position. If my goal with another Christian is unity, then my agenda becomes conformity. Either they will conform to my way of thinking or I will conform to theirs. If, however, I seek to love them, then unity will be the by-product of the relationship.

Sexuality

Most of the churches I know are wrestling with the issue of human sexuality. The Anglican Church has been engaged in a listening exercise for a few years now. Others, like the Baptist Union, are doing the same thing. If I am to be honest, I am not sure that a united opinion on the issue is possible. The challenge is that the subject has the potential to fracture the church. Working out whether Christian approaches to homosexuality are primary issues or secondary issues is complicated. Does it sit alongside issues such as those addressed by Paul in Romans 14 and 1 Corinthians 8? I am not sure it does. Does holding the view that living in a sexually active same-sex union is compatible with Scripture automatically mean you forfeit the right to describe yourself as a Christian? I am not so sure about that either. In many ways, I think unfortunately, human sexuality has become the touchpaper for unity in the church today.

One of the challenges the issue presents is that although it is a secondary issue it actually feels like it has primary significance. Of course, some may believe it to be a primary issue in and of itself, but I have a sense that the primary issues of Christian faith are those that are rooted in our credal confessions of who God is and what He has done in and through Christ to offer forgiveness and hope to the world. For many Christians, however, the way in which a fellow Christian engages with the issue of sexuality has become the central test of the way they view the Bible. For those who hold such a view, our understanding of sexuality has become the litmus test of our orthodoxy.

There are those who believe that it is equally biblically valid to endorse a same-sex relationship as it is to say that a same-sex relationship is wrong. There seems to be a deep contradiction in these two views. Is the Bible unclear on the issue or has there been a change in how the Bible is read and applied? If the Bible is unclear, then there must be a recognition that the issue is genuinely a secondary issue and must remain in that category. If, however, the Bible is clear and the issue has become blurred because the Bible's teaching itself has been changed, then while the issue is a secondary one, the way in which it is being addressed is exposing a primary concern, namely the authority and role of the Scriptures in Christian life and the teaching of the church.

While I share the reservations and concerns of many other Christians, it worries me deeply that this issue has become the lens through which many people are seeking to establish the authenticity of another person's faith. I hold a conservative position on the issue and believe that active same-sex relationships are incongruent with the clear teaching of the Bible. I have close friends who disagree with me who are also Christians. Put bluntly, I believe my view is faithful to the clear instruction of the Scriptures and theirs is not, but they believe that their view is faithful to the clear instruction and direction of the Scriptures and mine is not. When we talk about the issue I am not neutral. I think the issue has huge significance for the moral and ethical witness of the church into our society. I want to challenge the claim to biblical validity of the understanding of this issue of those who endorse active same-sex relationships, without suggesting for one moment that their view on this one issue means that they are not Christians. I am not saying that I believe they are not Christians, but I am saying that I believe that *on this issue* their view does not align with the Bible's clear teaching. I also want to find a way of avoiding their view *on this specific issue* becoming a reason for dismissing their reading of the Bible on every issue. I don't want to diminish their faith, their conviction, or their integrity, but I do want to be able to discuss the issue of sexuality with them fully, frankly, and graciously.

On both sides of the discussion I have encountered men and women of grace and kindness and compassion. I have been blessed by the willingness to listen, to think, and to pray that I have seen in the lives of many of those who have adopted a position that support same-sex relationships and same-sex marriage in the church. I have also been blessed by the same traits of character that I have seen in the lives of many of those who adopt a more conservative position on the issue. Unfortunately I have also seen ungracious and ungodly responses and reactions *on both sides* of this debate. If it is wrong for those with a conservative position to use this issue alone to reject the validity of the faith of a brother or sister, then it is equally wrong for a Christian who holds a view that supports same-sex relationships and same-sex marriage to reject the validity of the faith of a person who holds a more traditional and conservative approach on the issue.

I continue to investigate this issue, to pray about it, to reflect on it, and to study the Scriptures as I seek to be faithful to Christ in this area of my teaching and pastoral ministry. I have found a number of resources helpful in that process. Changing Attitude[42] is a group that works for the full inclusion of gay, lesbian, bisexual, and transgender people in the life of the Anglican Communion and has a list of books, resources, blogs, and comments that contain some really well-presented and thought-through arguments on the issues involved. Accepting Evangelicals[43] is an open network of evangelical Christians who believe the time has come to move toward the acceptance of faithful, loving same-sex partnerships at every level of church life, and the development of a positive Christian ethic for lesbian, gay, bisexual, and transgender people. They too have some helpful reflections, articles, and blogs on the issues involved. Living Out[44] is a website facilitated by a group of people who want to help Christian brothers and sisters who experience same-sex attraction to stay faithful to a more traditional understanding of biblical teaching on sexual ethics and to flourish at the same time. They also want to help the Christian church to understand how they can better help those who experience same-sex attraction to flourish. The Evangelical Alliance[45] also has some helpful resources on the issues, which can help local churches to think through the questions and form a coherent and compassionate response.

Of course, it is vital for us to personally engage directly in the best arguments on both sides of this discussion rather than settling for an argument presented to us by someone else. I found many of the resources addressing this discussion thoughtful, compassionate, and intellectually rigorous. For me, the challenge on the issue is really quite simple: despite a whole plethora of scholarship exploring human sexuality, I am yet to be persuaded by a strong and clear biblical argument in favour of same-sex relationships or same-sex marriage. It is for this reason that I continue to hold a conservative position on the issue, and it is also for this reason that I am unable to argue that both sides of the discussion have an equally biblical case. Of course, I recognize that those who sit on the other side of this debate would robustly disagree with me. I want to be able to have that discussion in a context of good disagreement, listening well to one another, understanding one another, and being honest and open and gracious with one another, but I still want the argument to be rooted in the text of Scripture and the ethical and moral centre of God's plans and purposes for men and women.

Whilst the issue itself is secondary, the way in which it is dealt with falls into a primary category. Some see sexuality itself as a primary, defining issue. Others, like me, see it is as a secondary issue but one that has significant importance and impact on the work and witness of the church. It is an issue that points to a greater disagreement which itself may lead to division. In my view, the debate about sexuality is actually a symptom of a greater challenge, and that greater challenge is the reliability and the authority of the Bible and how we approach it as Christians. I don't want to suggest that this is the only lens of understanding how someone approaches the Scripture, but I do want to acknowledge that it is one of the lenses by which we can do that. I don't think those with a different reading of Scripture on this issue can be labelled as unbiblical in every area of their lives because of their view on sexuality, but I do believe that it is right to question whether or not their reading of the Scriptures on this issue is a faithful one. Of course, they would say exactly the same thing about me, but in reverse. In Pauline terms, is the issue of sexuality to be treated like the holiness issues of eating meat offered to idols or the observance of a special day, or is it not?

In one sense, I do not think it can be treated like the issues of Romans 14 and 1 Corinthians 8. That is because to me this is not a justice issue; it is an issue of authority, holiness, and morality. How we deal with it should be shaped by our understanding of the Bible's teaching on holiness, morality, faithfulness, human flourishing, and the clear instructions of God to His people on how to live well. I want to warn my friends who disagree. I want to persuade them to see the issue differently. I am standing with a deep sense of conviction and I believe it is my responsibility to urge them to think again and to change their mind. They, on the other hand, also have a deep sense of conviction. They want to urge me to think again. Where I believe they are missing the clear teaching of Scripture on this issue, they believe I am missing the heart of God on the issue. I believe the clear direction of the whole of the Old and the New Testaments on human sexuality points to sexual activity being a gift that is blessed within the relationship of marriage between a man and a woman exclusively. The marriage image reflects the image of intimacy and union that Christ has with His church. It is holy, sacrosanct, and beautiful. Of course, my friends who disagree with me also think exactly the same way about my view. They want to change my mind. Neither side is neutral on the issue.

What if this is an issue unlike Romans 14?

Those who hold different views can love God deeply and be part of His kingdom. It is possible to sit on either side of arguments around human sexuality and still be a Christian. That does not mean that I can endorse the views of those who support same-sex marriage as equally biblically justified or justifiable. I want to hold the Scriptures open and invite a robust, feisty, passionate discussion on the issue with those who disagree with me. I want the discussion to be deeply embedded in the Scriptures and profoundly shaped by the direction and boundaries of the overarching biblical story. That position is hard to maintain because human sexuality is an incredibly important subject upon which I profoundly disagree with those who seek to present same-sex relationships as a credible and approved lifestyle choice biblically, because they obviously profoundly disagree with me on the issue too. But I also refuse to question their entire salvation or standing before God because we disagree. I believe it is a fundamental error to let the issue of sexuality become the new litmus test for Christian faith. I also think we should resist attempts to make it the litmus test for biblical orthodoxy generally. It should be possible to argue that someone whose view differs from ours on a secondary issue because it is not congruent with a clear reading of the Bible can be described as having an unbliblical view of that issue without jumping to the general statement that they are therefore an unbiblical person. We can disagree on this without rejecting one another completely.

Not all Christians have the same view about the Bible. I struggle when someone who endorses same-sex relationships and same-sex marriage asks me to describe their view as biblical because to me it seems to contradict the clear teaching of Scripture. I am not saying that I believe that they are unbiblical in everything, but I am saying that I believe that their view of this issue appears to be unbiblical. In such circumstances, the issue of sexuality has exposed the deeper issue of biblical authority and how it works itself out in our lives. That means I can acknowledge that the person with whom I disagree is a Christian, but I cannot describe their view of this issue as biblical in the straightforward sense of the word, and to my mind that means that they may have moved away from the roots of evangelical Christian faith and its historical roots. In a sense I understand that my personal stance, which I have set out here, could be seen to be a cause of division, but it is a division that flows from a desire to stand for the truth of Scripture, for the authenticity of the faith of the person with whom I disagree, and the need to be honest and open with one another.

The unity that Christ prays for in John 17 is rooted in truth. It demands a rigorous commitment to the truth on one side and a relentless commitment to love one another on the other. So I must love my brother or sister enough to challenge them, and I must love them enough to be challenged by them. I must allow for the possibility that agreement will not be possible. In questioning their commitment to biblical authority I am not questioning their salvation, but I am questioning their understanding of obedience and faithfulness to Scripture. I must also allow for the possibility that I might be wrong, and they might be right.

What if this is an issue like Romans 14?

In another sense, the issue is comparable to the issues addressed by Paul in 1 Corinthians 8 and Romans 14. The trajectory of that argument, however, is that I am the weaker brother and those who see nothing wrong with same-sex relationships are the stronger. In that case, it seems to be that the biblical instruction is aimed at the person who is engaged in the practice that is causing offence or concern. Paul makes it clear that those whose conscience is clear should avoid the disputed lifestyle for the sake of those who think it is wrong. Either way, unity is not achieved simply through defiant acquiescence. Unity is achieved through remembering that we are family.

It seems to me that there are two bigger issues at stake that sit underneath all the possible fracture points in the church today. From human sexuality to the role of men and women in the church, from denominational distinctiveness within the Protestant traditions to the relationship between the Roman Catholic Church and the rest of Christ's body, the key issues are whether or not we believe in Christ through the word of the Apostles, and whether or not we believe that if we do, then we are a family. We may approach that word with different understandings, but if we claim to place it at the centre of our understanding of who Christ is, who God is, and what His purposes are for the world, then we must be willing to grapple with the Bible together, in loving, passionate discourse and in mutual respect. And that mutual respect includes the possibility that someone might think there are biblical grounds (on either side of the argument) when there are actually not. If we love one another then we have to be able to have those difficult discussions. The raging battle in the church of Jesus Christ is a single battle with two key issues at its heart: firstly, is the word we believe the word of Christ given to the Apostles and given to us; and secondly, is the body of Christ a family? Christ prayed that all who believed in Him through the Apostles' word would be one. Isn't that the two issues in one prayer? All other discussions are symptoms of fissures on these two things.

Perhaps there is a lesson for us in how to approach this issue from a statement issued by senior British Baptists in December 2016.[46] While the statement is profoundly helpful for those of us who lead Baptist churches, there are many aspects of it that are also incredibly helpful for the wider Christian church. Consider this aspect of the call to unity as we wrestle with the issues of human sexuality:

We do not pretend that this will be easy. It will be costly. It will take time and effort that could be given elsewhere. It will involve our churches making themselves vulnerable at deep points. It will require churches to live with tensions and disagreements that some will find close to unbearable. We believe, however, that however protracted, painful, and precarious this existence might be, it is in fact our only place of true safety and security, because it is the place where God is calling us to live.

There will be churches amongst us who believe the demands of justice for LGBT+ people are so urgent that they will wish to resist this call to conversation and co-existence; there will be other churches who believe their own contextual mission will be so compromised by any re-examination of marriage that they will also want to resist. We call both sets of churches to have patience with those churches that are not yet so certain, to walk with them and help them to know better Christ's ways, despite the cost that comes with such patience.

There may be other churches on either side who will be uninterested in further conversation because they cannot imagine how a position other than their own could be faithful or biblical. To such we say, gently but seriously, that the limits of your – or our – imagination are not a good source of theological insight. The gospel call remains to be transformed by the renewing of our minds, to discover that sometimes, often, God gives more than we can imagine. The smallness of our imaginations can never be a reason to denigrate God's gifts.

Amongst the authors of this statement are some who believe that a properly Baptist engagement over sexual ethics will lead our churches to re-assert that male-female marriage is the only Christian way and others who believe that it will lead *our churches to embrace same-sex marriage as a profoundly Christian option. We talk about these things in private, and (some of us) in very public spaces too. We do not expect to convince each other any time soon, but in maintaining our friendships, learning from each other, and discovering more of the missional contexts and biblical insights that make us advocates for our differing positions, we encourage each other to follow Christ more faithfully even as we disagree. This, we believe, is our Baptist way.*

Shallow unity will avoid the question and paper over the cracks. Shallow unity will seek peace and harmony over truth and conviction. Aggressive fundamentalism will dismiss the conversation, disregard the views of those with whom it disagrees, and refuse to listen. What would biblical unity look like? It will keep the Bible open and keep a commitment to robust and challenging love even more open. It will wrestle, discuss, debate, argue, and interrogate the issue. It will refuse to deny a place in the family of God to those with whom it disagrees, even if it is unable to bless their view or participate in rites and rituals that do so. It will not sacrifice truth on the altar of grace, but nor will it sacrifice grace on the altar of truth. It may, in the end, recognize that staying together in a broken and fallen world is not possible. If it does, then the separation itself must become a gift to the world around us. Above all, it will remain rooted in Christ, tuned to His example; it will continue to love those brothers and sisters from whom it is separated and pray for a new revelation of faith love and hope because, in the end, love never gives up, even as it questions the biblical validity of their point of view on a particular issue.

4. The picture of our unity – like the relationship between the Father and the Son

The unity described in John 17:21 recognizes the deep connections between the Father and the Son, and Jesus prays that such deep connections will also be seen in the unity shared between those who follow God through Christ by the power of the Holy Spirit. Jesus actually prays that all believers will be "in" both the Father and the Son. The structure of the prayer in verse 21 is very similar to the structure of the prayer in verse 23:

> "That they may all be one. As you, Father, are in me and I am in you, may they also be in us, so that the world may believe that you have sent me."
>
> John 17:21

> "I in them and you in me, that they may become completely one, so that the world may know that you have sent me and have loved them even as you have loved me."
>
> John 17:23

The four parts of the prayer seen in both verses are easily identifiable:

1. The Father is in Christ.

2. Christ is in the Father.

3. That all believers may be in the Father and the Son.

4. So that the world might believe that the Father sent the Son.

Jesus prays that His followers will be one and then that they will be "in" the Father and the Son just as the Father and the Son are "in" one another. We see this kind of language in various places in John's writing:

> "Abide in me as I abide in you. Just as the branch cannot bear fruit by itself unless it abides in the vine, neither can you unless you abide in me. I am the vine, you are the branches. Those who abide in me and I in them bear much fruit, because apart from me you can do nothing. Whoever does not abide in me is thrown away like a branch and withers; such branches are gathered, thrown into the fire, and burned. If you abide in me, and my words abide in you, ask for whatever you wish, and it will be done for you. My Father is glorified by this, that you bear much fruit and become my disciples. As the Father has loved me, so I have loved you; abide in my love. If you keep my commandments, you will abide in my love, just as I have kept my Father's commandments and abide in his love. I have said these things to you so that my joy may be in you, and that your joy may be complete."
>
> John 15:4–11

> We declare to you what we have seen and heard so that you also may have fellowship with us; and truly our fellowship is with the Father and with his Son Jesus Christ.
>
> 1 John 1:3

What on earth can this mean for our understanding of unity? Leon Morris argues that the ideal of unity for which Jesus prays in John 17 is one in which believers increasingly recognize their dependence on God, rely upon their position in God, and witness to the intimacy and unity of God. He writes:

This does not mean that the unity between the Father and the Son is the same as that between believers and God. But it does mean that there is an analogy. The Father is in the Son and does His works (14:10). The Son is in the Father. The two are one (10:30) and yet are distinct. So in measure it is with believers. Without losing their identity they are to be in the Father and Son. Apart from the Son they can do nothing (15:5). In other words, the unity for which He prays is to lead to a fuller experience of the Father and the Son.[47]

C. K. Barrett goes further. He suggests that just as the Father works through the Son so we, as believers, must let the Father and the Son work through us. A failure to do so would render our witness and our ministries both meaningless and powerless. He argues that the way John includes this prayer would suggest that the issue of division and disunity was already a problem. Barrett suggests that John does not care about institutional unity very much at all. It is much deeper and more profound than that because it is a unity of heart, mind, and purpose, not just form and function:

The church's unity is not merely a matter of unanimity, nor does it mean that the members severally lose their identity. The unity of the church is strictly analogous to the unity of the Father and the Son; the Father is active in the Son – it is the Father who does his works (14:10) – and apart from the Father the deeds of the Son are meaningless, and indeed would be impossible; the Son again is in the Father, eternally with him in the unity of the Godhead, active alike in creation and redemption. The Father and the Son are one and yet remain distinct. The believers are to be, and are to be one,

*in the Father and the Son, distinct from God, yet abiding in
God, and themselves the sphere of God's activity (14:12).*[48]

The impact of this imagery and these words are profound. Jesus
prays that all believers would be united in the way that He is
to His Father. Just the briefest of reflections on the depth of
shared loved, mutual acceptance, and common purpose within
the relationship of God with Himself should cause us to stop
in wonder at this prayer. Is this truly what Christ wants for us,
this depth of commonality and mutual commitment? It seems
clear from the text that this is, indeed, what Christ is asking His
Father to do in us. I am struck by the little phrase at the very end
of Barrett's quotation, that believers are to become "themselves
the sphere of God's activity". We are not only a witness to the
world in what we do or in our mission and activity; we are also
a witness to the world in who we are and how we behave toward
one another.

I remember someone saying to me years ago that we do not
have a choice about whether we are theologians. We have no choice
but to be theologians when we are Christians because theology,
in its most straightforward definition, is words and ideas about
God. The same is true of our behaviours and attitudes toward one
another. We are a witness to God in how we treat one another
in Christ's church. The penetrating and unsettling question is
whether we are a good witness or a bad witness. Could the world
look at us and see the unity and intimacy of God in the way we
behave toward one another? Could they look at us and exclaim,
"Behold how these Christians love one another!"? William Barclay
puts it this way:

What was that unity for which Jesus prayed? It was not
a unity of administration or organization. It was not in
any sense an ecclesiastical unity. It was a unity of personal
relationship. We have already seen that the union between
Jesus and God was a union of love and obedience. It was a
unity of love for which Jesus prayed. It was unity in which
men loved each other because they loved Him. It was a unity
based entirely on the relationship between heart and heart.[49]

Jesus is praying for what would come to be known as the one, holy,
catholic, and apostolic faith. That is to say His body on earth across
all the continents and countries of the world throughout time who
would come from different cultures, stand in different traditions,
worship in different ways, use different words, and be part of
(sadly) different denominations, but it would be united around
the purpose and the work of the Lord Jesus Christ as described
to us through the preaching and the teaching of the Apostles and
contained in the Scriptures and passed down to us faithfully. This
is not merely a formal arrangement that is achieved through the
recitation of words that have been learned by rote without their
meaning being powerfully embedded in our hearts. Nor is it
only the result of denominational allegiances and pacts with one
another. It is not just an outward thing. William Barclay's words
are worth consideration again. It is worth remembering that his
words were published in 1955, with the shadow and the pain of
the Second World War a very present memory for many:

It will never be that Christians will organize their Churches all
in the same way. It will never be that they will worship God
in all the same way. It will never be that they will all believe

precisely and exactly the same things. But the Christian unity is a unity which transcends all these differences, and joins men together in love. The cause of Christian unity at the present time, and indeed all through history, has been injured and violated and hindered, because men loved their own ecclesiastical organizations, men loved their own creeds, men loved their own ritual, more than they loved each other. If we really loved each other and really loved Christ no man would ever be excluded from any Church, and no Church would exclude any man who was Christ's disciple. Only love implanted in the hearts of men by God can tear down the barriers which men have erected between each other and between their Churches.[50]

The astonishing truth is that the unity for which Jesus prayed in John 17 is founded upon, and supposed to mirror, the relationship of love between the Lord Jesus Christ, who is the Son of God, and His Father. This beautiful image picks up part of Jesus' moving address to His disciples from earlier in John. It probably took place earlier the same evening, so the words of Jesus would have been much fresher in the minds of those who heard Him pray this prayer than they are in ours. It is easy for us to allow them to become disconnected from one another, but it would have been much more difficult for His first disciples to have let that happen. As they heard Jesus pray the prayer we have in John 17 they would have remembered what He had said earlier:

> *"I give you a new commandment, that you love one another. Just as I have loved you, you also should love one another. By this everyone will know that you are my disciples, if you have love for one another."*
>
> John 13:34–35

It is easy for us to turn any discussions or explorations of unity into a bland and arid subject full of minutiae of behaviour and assurances of equality and mutual respect. It is worth remembering that these words are the last words of Jesus to His disciples. He has watched them fight about who was the greatest and the most important, and waited expectantly for one of them to rise from the table and wash His feet, but none of them was willing to move. In the heat of their discussions, and perhaps in their longings for Messianic deliverance, they forgot the basic call of God upon them, which was to love one another. So Jesus rose from the table and washed their feet. They were busy with discussion while He was busy with love. He speaks to them of loving one another, of being one, on the same evening as He explains His impending betrayal, torture, and death. He speaks to Judas, who would betray Him, and to Peter, who would deny Him, and to all the disciples who would run away from Him. In the midst of the worst evening of His life, He reminds them that they are to love one another and He asks His Father to make them one. Surely John would have remembered these words for the rest of His days on earth? Perhaps that is why He gave Himself to the church and the purposes of Christ so fully: He saw His Saviour model love and commitment and He heard His Saviour pray for mutual love, commitment, and honour in His body.

Most Christians have experienced this beautiful unity in one way or another. Sometimes it feels like music being played in another room. We meet others who are followers of Jesus and we know that their lives are given to the same Great Conductor. We wonder why on earth we have not spent more time allowing our melody to rise together. Sometimes we sense it when we meet Christians from other traditions or continents. I have been privileged to find this beautiful gift of unity in countries all around the world. I have sensed that I am one with brothers and sisters who live in the slums of Bangladesh, the palaces of England, the shanty towns of South Africa, the jungles of Cambodia, and the megachurches of the United States of America. Christians from totally different backgrounds, traditions, and cultures who somehow know that we are all one in Christ Jesus (Galatians 3:28) are given the gift of a beautiful family that is always growing and expanding. Sadly, we often miss this gift because we are afraid to reach out a hand of fellowship and love or to take the hand of someone whose traditions are so different from ours that we allow suspicion instead of love to win the day. This unity cannot be forced, manipulated, or coerced. It may be commanded but it cannot be commandeered. Yet surely the reality is that in a world which is as divided as ours is now, there can be absolutely no excuse for Christians to refuse to give ourselves afresh to see the unity that Jesus prayed for displayed to all around us. In the words of Tom Wright:

> *If we are, essentially, one in faith, there can be no final reason why we may not be one, also, in our life and worship.* [51]

5. The purposes of our unity – that the world might know the Son and the Father and that we might see Christ's glory

> *"... so that the world may believe that you sent me... so that the world may know that you have sent me."*
>
> John 17:21, 23

The purposes of the prayer of Jesus for unity are like a coin with two sides. On one side is the result of Christian unity for the people of the world who do not believe that the Lord Jesus Christ was sent by His Father. On the other side of the coin is the result of unity among Christians for Christians themselves. With regard to the purpose of Christian unity for those in the world who do not believe, Jesus prays that all who will believe in Him will be one so that the world might know that the Father has loved the Son and has sent Him. The very title of this book is based on this aspect of the prayer of Jesus. Jesus was not praying for unity for the sake of unity. He was not even praying for unity for the sake of truth. He prayed for unity for the sake of the world. His cry to His Father was that His disciples, in their united life, action, and witness, would as one body point to the greatest truth of all, that in Christ God was reconciling the world to Himself (2 Corinthians 5:20). Our unity points to His exclusive claims to be the Saviour of the world, the One who brings the face of the Father before us in His face. As we stand together, we do so to point to God Himself, the One who has made a way for all people to know Him. In a world where the exclusive claims of Christ are questioned and in a church that can often feel either afraid or embarrassed by this truth, it is vital to remember that Christ's prayer for our unity is that the world might know Him and His Father. There is no other way to know God fully and completely other than through the Lord Jesus Christ. This is the offensive claim of Christ that challenges modern pluralism, upsets many in the ecumenical world, and yet sits at the heart of the prayer of Jesus for His people.

One for All, the title of this book, is a phrase originally penned in the famous book *The Three Musketeers* by Alexandre Dumas. The story is set in 1625–28 and recounts the adventures of a young man named d'Artagnan, who travels to Paris to join the Musketeers of the Guard. D'Artagnan is not able to join them immediately, but he befriends the three most formidable musketeers, Athos, Porthos, and Aramis, and he becomes involved in affairs of the state and court. At times in the story it feels like the four central characters are continually facing hostility and challenge. It is in that context that the motto for their group emerges: "All for one and one for all, united we stand divided we fall."

The title of this book was chosen because it captures what we are trying to say about unity on a lot of different levels. Firstly, Christ Himself is the "One" who has died for all. The Apostle Paul expresses this when he writes to the believers in Rome:

> *Therefore just as one man's trespass led to condemnation for all, so one man's act of righteousness leads to justification and life for all. For just as by the one man's disobedience the many were made sinners, so by the one man's obedience the many will be made righteous.*
>
> Romans 5:18–19

Secondly, Christ has died once for all. He does not need to repeat his sacrificial death on the cross. We will never need another sin offering because Christ Himself has become the Great Sin Offering for all. His death has reconciled to God all who will turn to Him through Christ. Paul, once again writing to the Roman believers, speaks of the sacrifice of the Lord Jesus:

> *The death he died, he died to sin, once for all; but the life he lives, he lives to God.*
>
> Romans 6:10

The writer of the book of Hebrews states:

> *And just as it is appointed for mortals to die once, and after that the judgement, so Christ, having been offered once to bear the sins of many, will appear a second time, not to deal with sin, but to save those who are eagerly waiting for him.*
>
> Hebrews 9:27–28

Thirdly, there is a sense in which the title of the book captures the purpose of unity for the church of Jesus Christ. We are one for the world. We are united to display God's glory and to point people back to the Father who loves them enough to send His Son to the cross, and to the Son who loves them enough to die for them on that cross so that they can be brought into the Father's family, the Son's bride, the church of the Lord Jesus Christ. We are not united just to bless one another, and we are not united for the sake of unity itself. We are united so that the world might know the Father through the faithful ministry of the Son.

We hear this ultimate purpose echoed in the words of Jesus when He prays that His disciples might share in His glory:

> *"The glory that you have given me I have given them, so that they may be one as we are one… Father I desire that those also, whom you have given me, may be with me where I am, to see my glory."*
>
> John 17:22, 24

This unity is in itself a powerful witness to the purposes and the plans of God. Perhaps that is because it is more natural for people to be divided than it is for them to be together? Perhaps it is because we, as Christians, have allowed our default position to become one of separation rather than unity? The type of unity for which Christ prayed and to which we are called would itself be supernatural and therefore require a supernatural explanation.[52] It is an indictment upon us as Christians that when the world is faced with the disunity of Christians and churches, that disunity itself hinders them from seeing the supreme value of Christian faith. Our disunity puts people off.

It is not the size or scale of the church that draws people to Christ; it is the central unity of our message and mission. The Father and the Son are the single lynchpin of our unity. When we place God at the centre of our lives and our churches, we are able to celebrate other Christians and other churches and work more effectively with them.

That we might see Christ's glory

"Father, I desire that those also, whom you have given me, may be with me where I am, to see my glory, which you have given me because you loved me before the foundation of the world."

John 17:24

The other side of the coin for the purpose of our unity is explained in this verse. It is that those who are Christians might see the glory that the Father has given to Christ. Once again, the idea of Christ's people being with Him and sharing with Him is an image that we have seen before in John's Gospel:

"Whoever serves me must follow me, and where I am, there will my servant be also. Whoever serves me, the Father will honour."

John 12:26

"And if I go and prepare a place for you, I will come again and will take you to myself, so that where I am, there you may be also."

John 14:3

Jesus prays that His followers will be with Him and that they will see His glory. They are to know and to experience the reality that the Father has glorified the Son as the Saviour of the world and that the Son, who humbled Himself and made Himself obedient to the cross, has now been exalted to His rightful, permanent, and unbreakable position as the Sovereign of the world (Philippians 2). This prayer is for followers of Christ to see Jesus in His reinstated place of splendour and glory after He has lived among them. In a sense, it feels to me like a prayer that we will all have the chance to see something of the glory that Peter, James, and John saw on the Mount of Transfiguration (see Mark 9). This is not a glory given to the Son after He came to the earth in the form of Jesus. Rather it is the eternal glory of the Son now seen in the resurrected Lord Jesus Christ. Jesus asks His Father that all of Christ's followers will see this. That is something that I am very much looking forward to! In the end, the church of Jesus Christ will be reunited visibly with her Head and we will never be parted. We will one day see the glory of Christ as part of the Godhead.

6. The passion behind our unity – God's love

"Righteous Father, the world does not know you, but I know you; and these know that you have sent me. I made your name known to them, and I will make it known, so that the love with which you have loved me may be in them, and I in them."

John 17:25–26

As we come to the end of the prayer of Jesus in John 17, we see that the driving force behind His prayer is not power, glory, or sovereignty. More important than all of these is love, because God Himself is love and love is the motivation that sits at the heart of all He is and all He does. The Apostle John would later write some of the most powerful words in the Bible about this reality:

> *Beloved, let us love one another, because love is from God; everyone who loves is born of God and knows God. Whoever does not love does not know God, for God is love. God's love was revealed among us in this way: God sent his only Son into the world so that we might live through him. In this is love, not that we loved God but that he loved us and sent his Son to be the atoning sacrifice for our sins. Beloved, since God loved us so much, we also ought to love one another. No one has ever seen God; if we love one God, God lives in us, and his love is perfected in us.*
>
> 1 John 4:7–12

In the end, Jesus brings His prayer for unity to a conclusion by rooting it in the love of God. He describes the love of the Father that surrounds Jesus and this same love as the binding tissue of Jesus' disciples to God. It is through this love that the Father sent the Son in the first place, and it is this love that binds them to the Father and the Son to them and them to one another.

It is worth noting that the Father, who is described as holy in verse 11, is now, in verse 25, described as righteous. It is the only place that this phrase appears. Jesus does not need any favours from His Father; He knows that the will of the Father is perfect because He Himself is perfect and He has come to do that will. Jesus declares at the close of His prayer that, in the end, He desires to do the right thing. Jesus does not appear to be asking for anything here. He knows that those who know the Father will see Him as righteous and loving and that those who do not know Him may not see that, but it does not change the reality of who God is. The perfect will of the Father is seen in the perfect obedience of the Son.

God's will for the world and His will for the church is not rooted in some kind of egotistical control. It is not the product of a tyrannical deity who plays games with the future of His creation. It is rooted in His righteousness, and His righteousness itself is an expression of His love. It feels poignant to me that Jesus is declaring these truths in prayer here, on the night of His betrayal. Christ will feel the lash of the righteousness of God in the twenty-four hours that follow this petition. He will be nailed to a cross and the Trinity will endure a powerful moment in which God Himself, the righteous Father, and God the Son, holy and compassionate, make a way for those who are not righteous and not loving to become righteous and loving through Jesus Christ. The commitment of God to the world is inexplicable. His grace is beyond comprehension. His love is beyond question.

The implications of John 17

Firstly, through the prayer of Christ we have learned the parameters of His petition, namely that He includes every single believer. Exclusion is easier than the powerful truth that all who call on the name of Christ are united as brothers and sisters.

Secondly, we have seen that this prayer means that we ourselves as followers of Christ will face hard choices and difficult conversations if we are to see the prayer of Jesus answered and that answer demonstrated to the world. Schism is easier than division. Parting is sometimes the cowards' way out.

Thirdly, we have seen that the unity Christ prays for is the unity that is modelled in the perfect coordination and agreement of will and purpose that exists within the Godhead itself. This is surely harder to remain committed to than anything else in the prayer, because it is impossible in our own strength and wisdom. It is easier to claim that this is an idealistic request to be fulfilled in the future than it is to see it as a prayer that we can be part of answering in our own lives, communities, and nations.

Fourthly, we see the profoundly moving picture of the Father and the Son as the illustration and illumination of the unity for which Jesus prays. This picture drives me to my knees as I think of the ways in which I have failed to reflect this kind of love to my brothers and sisters in the family of God.

Fifthly, we see that the purpose of this unity is so that the world might know that the Father has sent the Son. So often we have settled for a lesser form of unity. A unity of organization or words but not of heart and of purpose will never achieve Christ's purposes and will, instead, become an obstacle. Our attitudes toward one another, themselves supposed to be gifts to the world, have become hindrances and obstacles. The one, holy, catholic, and apostolic church has, in its splintering and factions, become an intellectual hurdle to many that God Himself is loving, gracious, and kind.

Lastly, we have seen that the power behind this unity is love itself which is manifested in the relationship of Father and Son within the Godhead and is modelled in the Son's love for us as His children. What if the church could actually behave as one family in the way that Jesus prays we will in John 17?

Reflection

What if this prayer were to be answered in you and in me? What if the churches in Buckinghamshire, where I live, really understood the principles of this prayer and committed to living them out? What if we were to display the unity that God has given us rather than trying to attain it? What if God has already given unity as His gift to churches across the nations because there is actually only one church? I don't mean superficial unity. I mean heartfelt, Christ-inspired, Father-and-Son modelled, rooted-in-love unity that answers the prayer of Jesus for His people? What if Jesus' prayer is because He knows that we break this gift of unity rather than protecting it and that we are people prone to division and separation rather than unity and love? Is the unity that Jesus prays for in John 17 something that we have to strive to reach or is it something that God has given us?

Such a church would be a beautiful bride. She would be an attractive family. She would be a bold army. She would be a countercultural society. She would be the ultimate missional community. She would be a loving home. She would be a fruitful vine. She would be a profoundly challenging bulwark of truth. She would be a living witness to a living God. She would be an unstoppable force. God, may I see such a church arise in the world, in my nation, and in my community, and may the work begin in me.

This powerful picture of unity begins when we come to grips with the fact that the church of Jesus Christ is already one. This is not something we strive for; it is something we live from. To understand how that can be so, we need to turn our attention to the teaching of Paul to the Christians in Ephesus.

The Bedrock of Paul's Conviction - We are One

There is one body and one Spirit, just as you were called to the one hope of your calling, one Lord, one faith, one baptism, one God and Father of all, who is above all and through all and in all.

Ephesians 4:4–6

Has the prayer of Jesus in John 17 yet to be answered? Has Jesus' cry to His Father fallen on deaf ears? Some believe that the prayer remains unanswered because of our brokenness and the church's failure to be the people of God as He has called us to be. Others, like me, believe that the fundamentals of the prayer are being answered by God every time Christians find one another, love one another, and celebrate a shared faith and shared identity because we are already one in Christ. Unity is not something that we strive to create; it is something that we live from. We cannot make it, but we can break it. The great conundrum for Christians is that from God's perspective unity has been already been given to us as a gift, but from our perspective we see a divided and fractured church. We have fractured the unity that God has given us. We have broken the bond. If we are to see it restored we need to understand that we do not create unity; we preserve it. We have allowed division to be our status quo whereas

God's status quo is a united church. We find that unity by clearing the detritus of our divisions and allowing God's gift of unity to blossom again. The weeds of our distrust are choking the flowers of His gift of unity.

There are many ways in which the church of Jesus Christ is failing Him, and perhaps there is no clearer example than the ways in which we treat one another. The pain and distress that we can cause one another in the name of defending the truth is almost unbearable for many of us to watch. It is easy to understand why some people say that the Christian church is the only army that buries the wounded rather than caring for them. At the same time, however, we are capable of beautiful acts of unity and togetherness. The church in South Africa has been at the heart of building a new and beautiful picture of what unity can look like for a nation that is still deeply divided. As I write, the church in Dallas has risen to the challenge of racism, segregation, and separation to demonstrate a powerful picture of what a community that is united can look like. Many churches in Northern Ireland are finding ways of engaging across religious and cultural boundaries. Churches in networks such as Salt Box in Stoke-on-Trent are demonstrating what it looks like to be together in heart, mind, and purpose. Their unity is fostering new hope and new dreams in the city and bringing transformation to the wider region of Staffordshire.

What causes some churches to be so deeply divided while others can be so beautifully united? It is their core beliefs about the church, or ecclesiology, that shape the way they behave, and it has ever been thus.

Read the New Testament through just once, particularly the epistles, and you will be struck by how often it talks about the church. You could argue that it is one of the great themes of the letters generally and of Paul's letters in particular. He addressed many challenges through his writing to early Christian communities, and he almost always did so by drawing them back to the doctrine of the church. For example, what caused Paul to write to the Corinthian believers? We discover the answer very plainly:

> For it has been reported to me by Chloe's people that there are quarrels among you, my brothers and sisters. What I mean is that each of you says, "I belong to Paul," or "I belong to Apollos," or "I belong to Cephas," or "I belong to Christ."
>
> 1 Corinthians 1:11–12

His response to this division and schism is simple and profound: he reminds them of their essential unity in God, that the church of Jesus Christ is one community:

> Has Christ been divided? Was Paul crucified for you? Or were you baptised in the name of Paul?
>
> 1 Corinthians 1:13

Paul is crystal clear with the Corinthians that their divisions and schisms are the result of wrong thinking. They have misunderstood who they are and as a result have allowed themselves to form into little groups of individuals.

> Now I appeal to you, brothers and sisters, by the name of our Lord Jesus Christ, that all of you should be in agreement and that there be no divisions among you, but that you be united in the same mind and purpose.
>
> 1 Corinthians 1:10

Paul's letters to the Corinthians address issues of personality cults, doctrinal division, sexual immorality, confused thinking, spiritual snobbery, selfishness, pride, and one-upmanship. His epistle to the Galatians has to deal with legalism, narrow-mindedness, and attempts by believing Jews to make believing Gentiles behave like Jews. He addresses right doctrine and behaviour in Rome and in Ephesus. His missive to the Colossians addresses issues of spiritual superiority and confused thinking around angels. When he writes to the Philippians he addresses gossip and backbiting. When he writes to the Thessalonians he has to deal with their obsessive behaviour around the second coming of Christ and misunderstandings about life after death and the end of the world. James, the brother of Jesus, writes to encourage Christians who are facing persecution. Peter writes his two epistles to Christians who are struggling with rising opposition. John writes his three letters to those who need to be reminded of the centrality of the Lord Jesus and the importance of love. Yet every single one of them addresses their letters to people whom they describe as brothers and sisters. Their whole message is embedded in the conviction that the believers in Rome, Corinth, Galatia, Ephesus, Colossae, Philippi, Thessalonica, the Diaspora, and indeed all believers, are brothers and sisters. Read the number of times they speak of "our Lord Jesus Christ" or something similar. Paul writes to "all God's beloved in Rome, who are called to be saints" (Romans 1:7), referring to them as "brothers and sisters" at the end of the letter (Romans 16:17), and in Romans 16 he sends greetings to various churches and acts as a messenger of greetings from one church to another. He commends Phoebe, a minister of the church in Cenchreae (Romans 16:1). He notes his own thanks and the thanks of all the churches of the Gentiles for Priscilla and

Aquila and he mentions that they have a church in their home (Romans 16:4–5). He also goes through a large list of names of people from different places, cultures, and backgrounds (I count thirty-nine different people or groups in chapter 16 alone), and he brings his greetings to a close by saying, "All the churches of Christ greet you" (Romans 16:16).

Paul repeatedly identifies his recipients as a part of God's family:

> To the church of God that is in Corinth, to those who are sanctified in Christ Jesus, called to be saints, together with all those who in every place call on the name of our Lord Jesus Christ, both their Lord and ours.
>
> Grace to you and peace from God our Father and the Lord Jesus Christ.
>
> 1 Corinthians 1:2–3

> To the church of God that is in Corinth, including all the saints throughout Achaia:
>
> Grace to you and peace from God our Father and the Lord Jesus Christ.
>
> 2 Corinthians 1:1–2

> Paul an apostle… and all the members of God's family who are with me,
>
> To the churches of Galatia:
>
> Grace to you and peace from God our Father and the Lord Jesus Christ, who gave himself for our sins to set us free from the present evil age, according to the will of our God and Father, to whom be the glory forever and ever. Amen.
>
> Galatians 1:1–5

To the saints who are in Ephesus and are faithful in Christ Jesus:

> *Grace to you and peace from God our Father and the Lord Jesus Christ.*

Ephesians 1:1–2

To all the saints in Christ Jesus who are in Philippi, with the bishops and the deacons:

> *Grace to you and peace from God our Father and the Lord Christ.*

Philippians 1:1–2

Paul… and Timothy our brother,

> *To the saints and faithful brothers and sisters in Christ in Colossae:*
>
> *Grace to you and peace from God our Father.*

Colossians 1:1–2

To the church of the Thessalonians in God our Father and the Lord Jesus Christ:

> *Grace to you and peace .*

1 and 2 Thessalonians 1:1–2

Note how many times Paul uses the word "our" in his introductory remarks and greetings. Again and again he will go on to challenge their behaviour, their thinking, and their attitudes, but he always does so within the context of the family of God, reminding them from the outset that they are all part of one family. In fact, it is impossible to understand the way in which Paul does his theology without first understanding his ecclesiology. The appeals that Paul makes in his letters are always made within the context of his recipients being part of the church, the family of God. We would do well to remember that today. We are all part of the church. If we want to understand the teaching of the New Testament, this is one of the essential building blocks that we must get right. If we fail to understand that we are part of one church then the teaching and the instruction we receive from Scripture will fall on deaf ears. Perhaps this is, indeed, one of our great problems? We so often start with ourselves. We begin a discussion about faith and the role of Christian faith in the world with what we think, what we want, what we perceive to be true. We are far too subjective. Of course, such egocentricity is the result of our sinfulness because sin always causes us to put our own best interests first. When we compare that with the continual and steady flow of ecclesiology in the New Testament, however, we are confronted with a very different and somewhat liberating narrative. Words such as "me", "I", and "mine" become the words "we", "our", and "ours" in our discourse and thinking with one another.

One

The New Testament reminds us that we are part of something bigger, organically connected to the greater whole. We are members of the mystical body of Christ and are therefore inseparably tied to one another. If we understand this, then our approach to disagreement is changed and the tone of our words is inevitably altered. In the letter to the Ephesians Paul addresses the issue of unity again and again, and in chapter 4 he sets out a powerful narrative around unity and its implications for believers. One small phrase is nestled in Paul's letter to the Ephesians which contains the essence of this unity succinctly and acts as a bedrock for how we understand our unity. It is also found in chapter 4. Let me set the context before we examine the words themselves.

In chapters 1 to 3 of the letter Paul has set out the great spiritual inheritance of believers and the great change that has taken place in their status before Almighty God. He has reminded them of who they are in God by exploring the power of the Trinity at work in them (Ephesians 1:3–15). God the Father has chosen and blessed them in Christ and destined them for adoption into the family of God. God the Son has redeemed them through His death on the cross and has secured their forgiveness. He has shown them the depth of the Father's love and mercy. God the Holy Spirit has become their down payment of all that is to come and the sign of the inheritance they will enjoy. He sustains their hope and their anticipation of what is to come. Having explained all this to them, Paul then prays that they will understand these powerful truths.

He goes on to tell them that their previous religious, social, and cultural divisions have been swept away by the grace and mercy of God (Ephesians 2:1–10). The mutual hostility that existed between Gentiles and Jews has been destroyed. The middle wall of partition and segregation has been demolished and they are now part of a single new humanity, one new body, the church:

> *For he is our peace; in his flesh he has made both groups into one and has broken down the dividing wall, that is, the hostility between us. He has abolished the law with its commandments and ordinances, so that he might create in himself one new humanity in place of the two, thus making peace, and might reconcile both groups to God in one body through the cross, thus putting to death that hostility through it.*
>
> Ephesians 2:14–16

This monumental shift in their status is precisely why Paul himself is engaged in his ministry to the Gentiles (Ephesians 3:1–13), and he prays that the recipients of his letter might allow the change that has taken place in their standing before God to transform their experience of life and their understanding of God (Ephesians 3:14–21). His beating heart is that they would understand that all who are in Jesus Christ are already made one. This is not something that they strive for, reach out to attain, or make happen in their own strength or through their own ingenuity. They are one because Christ has made them one through His death and resurrection. If they do not understand this, they will never understand the colossal grace that has been shown to them. If they do not understand this, then their lives will continually be blighted with division, arguments, schisms, and suspicion. If they understand their new status, however, the way they view themselves and others will be fundamentally altered.

Ephesians 4

In Ephesians 4 these themes of unity, togetherness, singleness of purpose, and taking hold of what Christ has done for them are ringing in their minds. Paul does not ask them to become united; he pleads with them to live out of the reality of the unity that Christ has brought to them:

> *I therefore, the prisoner in the Lord, beg you to lead a life worthy of the calling to which you have been called, with all humility and gentleness, with patience, bearing with one another in love, making every effort to maintain the unity of the Spirit in the bond of peace.*
>
> Ephesians 4:1–3

Paul pleads with them to "maintain the unity of the Spirit in the bond of peace", not to establish it. He recognizes that this intention will be hard and urges them to be patient with one another, to be humble and gentle, and to constantly remember that this unity is what they are called to live out. You can hardly miss the importance of the truths he is setting before them and the passion with which he is pleading. He really needs them to understand this because to him, this unity of heart, this singleness of family that has been established by Christ for all His people, sits at the heart of Christian living.

We come now to the succinct summary statement of Ephesians 4:4–6. I believe that this short statement, alongside the words of Psalm 133, the prayer of Jesus in John 17, the declaration of Paul in 1 Corinthians 12:27, and his powerful announcement in Galatians 3:28, forms vital foundations for understanding the nature of Christian unity:

> *There is one body and one Spirit, just as you were called to the one hope of your calling, one Lord, one faith, one baptism, one God and Father of all, who is above all and through all and in all.*
>
> Ephesians 4:4–6

Paul strongly reinforces the idea of unity here by his repeated use of the word "one". In fact, he uses it seven times, prompting some to suggest that he is mirroring the idea of a perfect, God-given unity because of the associations of the number seven in Scripture. He also creates a strong sense of unity by repeatedly using the word "all". He reminds the Ephesian believers that God is the Father of all, above all, through all, and in all. Notice again that Paul does not suggest that any of the seven pictures that he paints are things yet to be achieved. They are all statements of fact. In the original language of this passage, the phrases do not have a verb. This has been added by translators to help us understand the gist of the words. If we were to translate it directly it would read as follows:

> *Doing absolutely everything you can with all your strength to protect and maintain the Spirit's unity in the bond of whole-life peace: one body and one Spirit, just as you were called to the one hope of your calling; one Lord, one faith, one baptism; one God and Father of all who is above all and through all and in all.*

What God has given them they are to protect and maintain above everything else. Paul sets out seven pictures of the unity that God has given them but does so by grouping them in a way that connects these pictures to the work of the Trinity itself:

Through God the Spirit:

1. One body;

2. One Spirit;

3. One hope.

Through God the Son:

4. One Lord;

5. One faith;

6. One baptism.

Through God the Father:

7. One God and Father of all who is above all and through all and
   in all.

Paul grounds their unity in the Trinity itself! He does not ground
it in good intentions or in naïve assumptions. He makes it clear
that maintaining this unity will be hard work. It will not be an easy
choice, but it is a vital one. He begs the Ephesians to remember
that this unity must sit at the centre of their lives and their sense
of Christian family and community. This unity must be guarded
above all else.

Is this the kind of priority that you and I give to Christian
unity? As I minister in various places across the world I am often
struck by the low priority that is given to Christian unity. It
sometimes feels like our default has become isolation and that we
will turn to unity as a last resort. I wonder what would happen if
we were to make unity our default. What if the position of every
local church was something like this: we will only work in isolation
when there is absolutely no way of working together; we will not
seek to do anything independently but will, instead, celebrate
the unity that God has given His church by looking for ways to
display His unity through how we speak about one another, how
we deliver our programmes, and how we describe ourselves.

One simple example of what this might look like would be
a sign I saw outside Greyfriars Church in Reading in Berkshire
many years ago. The church noticeboard described Greyfriars as
part of God's church in Reading. It was the oldest, most established
church in the town. It was also one of the largest. The church was
identifying itself, however, as part of the body of Christ in the

town. That is a beautiful sentiment and is quite a simple thing for every local church to do. Often churches do not have this mindset of standing as one.

Maybe the stumbling block is the effort that it takes? Maybe local churches feel so theologically at odds with other churches that they just cannot envisage any kind of partnership with them? Maybe local churches feel that they actually are better than other congregations? Maybe there is a sense in some local churches that it is easier to do things on our own? I recall a local church leader in my own area coming to meet me when he moved to the county and observing that none of the other churches seemed to be doing very much that was effective, and that was the reason he was not keen to work with them!

Whether it is fuelled by a desire to protect our theological purity, expediency, arrogance, or laziness, working in isolation has become the default position of local churches far too often. There may well be situations where we cannot work alongside others, but surely they should be few and far between and the exception to the rule rather than our default?

The way in which Paul sets out his pictures of unity deeply embedded in the work and the character of the Trinity for the Ephesian believers is very interesting. The standard approach to the Trinity is to speak of the Father, the Son, and the Holy Spirit, but Paul reverses this order here and speaks of the Spirit, the Son, and the Father. It is intriguing to consider what he does here. My view is that he is starting where the Ephesian believers are. He speaks first of the Spirit's work because that is the pragmatic thing to do. They have been brought together in the Spirit's power and their sense of purpose and meaning flows from the Spirit's work in them. This is where they find themselves. They are connected spiritually. That connectivity, however, is birthed out of the work of the Son, the Lord Jesus Christ. They believe in Jesus as their Lord. They have joined His family through the entry portal of baptism. Their trust is placed in Christ and what He has done for them. That is why the Spirit's work leads them to the Son. After all, isn't that what the Apostle John tells us the Spirit would do? In the Farewell Discourse (John 14–17), John records the Lord Jesus telling His disciples that the Spirit will point back toward Christ Himself and forward to the truth. The Spirit points them to the Son and the Son presents them to the Father.

Paul's reverse order will remind them of the gift that their unity is. It comes from God the Father, through God the Son, and is experienced by the power of God the Holy Spirit. From beginning to end, Christian unity is a work of God that is given to us and we are entreated to enjoy it and participate in it. By describing it in the way that he does, Paul also reminds the Ephesian believers of the opening thoughts of his letter to them. Unity is an expression of their faith, and their faith is a gift from God. Just as they are loved by the Father, redeemed by the Son, and sealed by the Spirit (Ephesians 1) so they are also united by the sealing work of the Spirit, united under the Lordship of the Son, and united in the family of God, the church.

Now let me turn our attention to what each of these seven pictures of Paul can teach us about the unity that we share.

Reflection

The unity that Paul describes in Ephesians 4 is so deeply rooted that it is inseparable from our understanding of us ourselves and the wider body of Christ. The deep challenge of this way of thinking for us is profound. We have so often allowed the default of division to become the way that we think rather than the default of unity. How can you and I begin to uproot the wrong thinking we have about unity and replace it with a healthier view? What difference does it make to your thinking to reflect on the fact that unity is already given to us in Christ and that our responsibility is not to create it but instead to preserve and protect it? Does it make it easier or harder to invest in unity? Perhaps the idea that our role is to remove the obstacles to unity is easier to apply to our lives and ministries than the idea that we are to create unity? What are the obstacles to this sense of being one in your church and your community? How can you remove those barriers? Can you become a prophetic voice for unity in your church and your community?

Think about the ways in which you can celebrate both the diversity and the unity of the church in your community. Could you think about drawing up a charter among the churches in your area? How can you work in mission together? Why not think about identifying the needs of the community and the strengths and weaknesses of each church and how you might work together in mission? What are the things that you could not do together? Are there reasons for that which can be addressed or are these deep-seated disagreements that you simply need to acknowledge and be honest about? How can you pray for one another and support one another in mission and in ministry? Why not make a list of the names of the leaders of the other churches in your area and commit to praying for them every week for a month or two? Or maybe you could ask your church family to pray for another church family every Sunday when you meet?

One Body – A Shared Family

Now you are the body of Christ and individually members of it.

1 Corinthians 12:27

The image of the Church as a body is one of Paul's favourites. Not only does he use it in his letter to the Ephesians, but he also uses it powerfully in his letter to the Corinthians and his letter to the Romans. In his letter to the Romans and his first letter to the Corinthians Paul uses the metaphor of a body to encourage them to avoid selfish behaviour and instead to remember that they have a relational and spiritual responsibility toward one another:

> *For the grace given to me I say to everyone among you not to think of yourself more highly than you ought to think, but to think with sober judgement, each according to the measure of faith that God has assigned. For as in one body we have many members, and not all the members have the same function, so we, who are many, are one body in Christ, and individually we are members one of another. We have gifts that differ according to the grace given to us: prophecy, in proportion to faith; ministry, in ministering; the teacher, in teaching; the exhorter, in exhortation; the giver, in generosity; the leader, in diligence; the compassionate, in cheerfulness.*

Romans 12:3–8

Paul then goes on to encourage the believers in Rome to love one another genuinely, to reject evil, and to love those who seek to hurt or harm them as Christians. Interestingly, this pattern of encouraging the believers to remember that they are a body and that they have each received different gifts from God followed by an encouragement to love one another deeply and be a good witness to the world around them is a pattern that is also used in both the Corinthian and the Ephesian passages. His detailed use of the language of the body in 1 Corinthians 12:12–31 is the most extensive use of the metaphor:

> *For just as the body is one and has many members, and all the members of the body, though many, are one body, so it is with Christ. For in the one Spirit we were all baptized into one body – Jews or Greeks, slaves or free – and we were all made to drink of one Spirit.*
>
> 1 Corinthians 12:12–13

Note the similar references to the Spirit and baptism here and in Ephesians 4.

In verses 12–26 of the chapter Paul illustrates the metaphor of the body and its importance by reminding the Corinthians of a number of different principles. Firstly, he points out that one part of the body cannot rule itself out of the whole because it feels inferior (verses 14–16). Secondly, he reminds them of the basic principle that a healthy body needs all of its constituent parts to function appropriately to maintain its health (verse 17). Paul then assures the believers in Corinth that God Himself has set the various parts of the body in the right places and that they need one another (verses 18–20). In verse 21 he reminds them that the more important parts of the body cannot dismiss as useless those parts that appear to be less important. He then goes on to point out that the parts of the body that seem to be less useful are actually vital and are given more honour because of how they are clothed and shielded (verses 22–24). In verses 25 and 26 Paul points out that the whole body should care for one another and that when one part of the body suffers, the whole body suffers, and when one part is honoured, the whole body is honoured. He then proceeds, "Now you are the body of Christ and individually members of it" (1 Corinthians 12:27).

In the remainder of the chapter Paul picks the image of various functions and offices given to the church for it to function well and encourages the believers in Corinth to function in their gifts and roles.

What we see in the summary statement of Ephesians 4 is that there is one body. In his other writing, Paul elucidates the implications of that. Reading the statement in Ephesians 4:4, I have the sense that Paul is emphasizing the powerful unity implications of the image of the body, whereas in both 1 Corinthians and Romans he is using the body image as a springboard into the mutual participation of the believers in the life of the church. Of course, he does this in Ephesians too, but the powerful seven-fold summary statement in verses 4 to 6 bring the mind to a sharp and distinctive focus around the organic and spiritual unity of the one body to which all Christians belong.

We can pull out the implications of this picture from the other two passages and other places in the writings of Paul. I find it helpful to reflect on one phrase from each of the three epistles I have mentioned, namely Ephesians, 1 Corinthians, and Romans, together:

There is one body.

Ephesians 4:4a

Now you are the body of Christ and individually members of it.

1 Corinthians 12:27

So we, who are many, are one body in Christ, and individually we are members of one another.

Romans 12:5

These writings from the early years of the church show me that there were already issues around unity for Christians. These words, coupled with the evidence I cited earlier from the general introductions and comments in so many of the epistles, demonstrate that disunity was a problem from very early on in the church. In fact, it would appear that issues of division appeared from as early as Acts 6, when there was dispute between two factions in the church in Jerusalem concerning the way in which widows and those in need were being cared for.

Paul's use of the image of the body in Ephesians 4 builds on his use of the image on two separate occasions earlier in the letter. In chapter 1 he reminds the Ephesian believers that Christ is the head of His body, the church, and in chapter 2 he reminds them that Christ has brought both Jews and Gentiles together into a new body through the cross:

And he has put all things under his feet and has made him the head over all things for the church, which is his body, the fullness of him who fills all in all.

Ephesians 1:22–23

He has abolished the law with its commandments and ordinances, so that he might create in himself one new humanity in place of the two, thus making peace, and might reconcile both groups to God in one body through the cross, thus putting to death that hostility through it.

Ephesians 2:15–16

Six aspects of what it means to be one body

1. The invisible church or the visible church?

What are we to make of this powerful picture of the church as one body? The first question we need to consider is whether this image refers to the invisible reality of the church as she is seen by God or whether it refers to the visible church on earth? The invisible church is a body of people made up of all those who trust and serve Christ no matter what part of the world they are in or what period of time they have lived. The visible church is all those people who have become part of an earthly community of Christians by joining a church, enlisting on its membership role, or affiliating themselves to it in one way or another. The former is made up of believers only and consists of every single person who has been born by God and brought into His family. The latter may include those who do not know Christ and have not trusted in Him. They may be members of a denomination but they are not actually members of God's family because they have not experienced the new life that Christ offers. Martyn Lloyd-Jones firmly believed that Paul was referring to the invisible church:

It is surely obvious that the Apostle must of necessity be referring to the mystical, unseen and spiritual Church. It cannot mean the visible and the external church for the good reason that the visible and external church consists of many bodies, a multiplicity of bodies. The Apostle was therefore not thinking of that. He is thinking of the essential Church, the mystical Church which is invisible, the mystical body of Christ.[53]

On the other hand, as we discovered in the earlier chapter entitled *We're Family*, the early church fathers such as Tertullian, Cyprian, and Augustine all argued that there could only be one organizational structure of the church on the earth. For a long time this difference of opinion has divided Roman Catholics and the rest of the Christian church, although it should be noted that for many years now Roman Catholicism has recognized the validity of the faith of Christians beyond the Roman Catholic structures. My own view is that while Martyn Lloyd-Jones is right to identify the image of one body as referring to the invisible church, expressing his conclusion with less strength might have been a better step. Paul would not have known other church structures when he wrote the letters to the Ephesians, the Romans, and the Corinthians. In Paul's understanding I am sure he was referring to one organizational unity called the church.

As time has passed and divisions have opened between different parts of the church of Jesus Christ, the concept of one body has come to include all those who have called on Christ on earth across continents, eras, and streams (and indeed all those who have come to Christ without ever being part of any Christian stream or denomination). For Paul, the only difference between the visible church and the invisible church was that there were those in the structures of the church on earth who had not come to faith in Christ. He did not have the challenges of denominational allegiances and affiliations to deal with. Our situation is different. Not only must we acknowledge that there are probably those in every Christian stream who have not actually come to a saving knowledge of Christ, but we must also recognize that amid the plethora of denominations and sections of the church there are people who know Christ and are part of His body despite being embedded in different structures and holding to many different secondary doctrinal beliefs. We are often too quick to disregard those who are part of a different stream to our own, and we are often also too quick to see the perfections in our own denominations and not the flaws. The one body to which Paul referred is made up of all who belong to Christ, whether they look and sound like us or agree with every point of our doctrine or not. Those who have been born anew by God are part of His family and therefore they are part of His body.

2. Organic unity

The second thing to note about the concept of this one body is that it is an organic unit. The only way into it is through new birth. It spans the centuries, the continents, and the cultures of the world. The New Testament sees the church of Jesus Christ as a new creation, and she is a new creation that has been brought into being by God Himself. Ephesians 2 reminds us of this very powerfully. God has not simply merged together believing Gentiles and believing Jews. He has formed "one new humanity" (Ephesians 2:15). This one new humanity is the one body of Christ, the church (Ephesians 2:16).

The image of the body helps us to understand this truth beautifully. How does a hand become a hand? How does an ear become an ear? They are not formed separately and then added to the emerging body in a mother's womb. Instead the hand, the ear, and every other part of the body grow from the single cell at the beginning of life. None of the parts of the human body ever existed on its own, and the parts do not have a life of their own. They are organically and permanently dependent upon the body itself for their life, the definition of their purpose, and their longevity. In the natural order of things, when the body dies, they die. It is true that transplants and modern medicine mean that one organ or part of a person's body can be transplanted into another person's body, but that is not the point of Paul's use of the image of the body. Firstly, transplantation did not exist, and secondly, the point he is making is that the body gives definition, life, and purpose to its parts. There is an essential and organic unity in the body. This is also true of the church of Jesus Christ.

We can put our names on as many church rolls and registers as we like without it meaning we are part of the church of Jesus Christ. To be part of the one body of Christ we must be born into it. We must find our life, our source, and our purpose through the vital, organic, and living relationship that God gives to all who are part of His family. To be part of the body is to be a partaker in the divine nature, to carry the DNA of God in our lives, to be born again, not according to natural methods but by the Spirit of God (John 3).

3. A diverse body

We must be careful not to allow the idea of the unity of the church to be translated into a rigid notion of uniformity. There is diversity in the unity of the church. The images that Paul uses are very obvious. In the picture of the human body he notes that there are hands, ears, feet, and so forth that are part of the human body. They are all part of the body but they have different functions. They share the same DNA but they have different roles. The same is true in the one body that is the church. In Ephesians, Corinthians, and Romans Paul follows the description of the church as a body by noting that there are different functions for different people within that body. Some are pastors, some are teachers, some are evangelists, some are prophets, some are apostles. He encourages every individual believer to find their role and their function in the body of Christ and to give themselves to fulfilling it passionately.

Uniformity in the church can so quickly lead to boredom and blandness. The church is so much healthier and so much more attractive when we allow her to be a place where the God-given gifts, talents, and passions of individual believers can be knit together for the glory of God. We are diverse, yet one. I find it deeply moving that Paul spends so much time in 1 Corinthians 12 reminding the believers in Corinth that those parts of the body that appear to be less important are actually vital. Each time I read those words I am reminded of the vital place of those with disabilities in the church of Jesus Christ and the terrible way in which they are often treated. If all those who live with a disability on the earth were counted as one people group they would be the poorest people on the earth, they would be the most discriminated against, they would be the least educated, they would be the most marginalized, and shockingly, they would be the least evangelized, the least discipled, and the group from which fewest leaders in the church would emerge. Surely that cannot be right? Our unity in diversity in the body of Christ means that we are not complete until all those who are part of Christ's family are represented in our congregations. Issues such as gender, race, citizenship, nationality, social standing, economic status, age, educational background, physical or mental ability, and so many more are all secondary. The body is not complete without every one of them being there. We are diverse, yet one.

4. Interdependent

We need one another in this one body. Not one of the parts of the body has a function and a life in and of itself. Its purpose and life flows from its place within the whole body. A foot is not a whole body. A hand is not a whole body. They cannot be. The same is true in the church of Jesus Christ. There is no independence in the body. We derive our meaning, our purpose, our significance, and our very essence from our relationship to the rest of the body. Not only do we need one another, but we also benefit from the presence of one another in the body. This is true not just in the local church of which we are part but also in the church in our town, our region, our nation, and our world. We are richer and more diverse and more beautiful together, and we rely on one another for the vastness of the demonstration of God's grace, power, and purpose in the world. No part is unimportant. Every single person who is part of the church of Jesus Christ is vital. We may not all stand on platforms, but we each have a part to play in extending the kingdom of God on the earth.

Between 2007 and 2010 I pastored a small local church in Berkshire. It is called Mortimer West End Chapel. It was a beautiful community of godly people. I loved my time with them and continue to think of them and pray for them often. While I was leading the church there were two wonderful examples of this sense of interdependence. The church building has been on the current site since 1798. It is adjoined to the manse and therefore it became my prayer room at times when it was not being used for other things. I remember once sitting in a pew at the back of the church and noticing some very old writing on the pew in front of me. It mentioned the names of people who had been part of the church in the early 1800s. No doubt they were bored teenagers who decided to mark their presence by etching something on to the pew. That wasn't the point. The point to me was that these people were part of this community of faith. They were part of the church. They contributed to it. They made a difference. They were needed. That thought encouraged me. I decided to thank God for those who had given their lives, their finances, and their talents to the church over the years. I walked round the outside of the building and as I did I saw the names of people etched on the bricks. They had obviously contributed to the building of the little chapel. Perhaps they played their part by physically placing the bricks there, or maybe their role was to pay for some of the materials. I do not know. It doesn't really matter. The point is they were unknown to me and unknown to nearly everyone in this generation, but they played their part. We would not be there, using that building and reaching that community, without them.

Local churches around the world are full of people who think they are unimportant. The opposite is true. They are vital. The role of leaders such as me and other pastors and teachers, prophets, evangelists, and apostles is to support our brothers and sisters for the work of the ministry. We exist because they do. Our role is to serve them, love them, release them, encourage them, and help them to be all that God wants them to be. We need each other.

The second example was the way in which the chapel (as we called it) worked with other local churches in the area to reach out to the community. None of the local churches was large, and none of them was wealthy. That did not stop us from trying to make a difference in the communities around us, however. We set up a missional group across the local churches called Christians Together in Mission. We discovered the strengths and weaknesses of each local church and the needs and wants of the communities around us, and we then began to meet the needs that we could and dream about how we might continue to grow our ministry and mission to the local communities. That interdependent ministry has continued to grow and flourish. The local churches now provide chaplaincy into a local school, a drop-in café for senior citizens, an annual fun day for the local community, a combined holiday Bible club for children each summer, and so many other things. All of it sprung from the recognition that the local churches were all part of the one body and that they needed one another. We were designed to be interdependent, and we work better when we work together.

5. We all share the same objective

Perhaps it is obvious, but a fifth impact of being one body is that we all share the same overarching aim. While we each have our own part to play in the body of Christ, the truth is that all of our individual contributions are given the overarching aim and objective of Christ's church. You cannot close a book with your kidney; neither can you pass water with your hands! The whole body is required for one purpose, which is healthy living.

The same is true of the church of Jesus Christ. It may seem obvious, but it is not unusual to see a church become caught up in the wrong purpose. The prayer warriors try to make the church only about praying. The evangelists try to make the church only about conversions. The teachers try to persuade everybody that the purpose of the whole church is teaching. Of course, they are all wrong. Earlier in his letter to the Ephesians, Paul has reminded them of the great purpose of God:

> *Although I am the very least of all the saints, this grace was given to me to bring the Gentiles the news of the boundless riches of Christ, and to make everyone see what is the plan of the mystery hidden for ages in God who created all things; so that through the church the wisdom of God in its rich variety might now be made known to the rulers and authorities in the heavenly places.*
>
> Ephesians 3:8–10

The overarching purpose of the church is to do the will of God, to see men and women won to Christ, discipled, and baptized. In the words of Habakkuk, the overarching purpose of God is that the glory of the Lord will cover the earth "as the waters cover the sea" (Habakkuk 2:14). This is the great, magnificent purpose of God on the earth, and it is the purpose of His people, the church. We each bring our gifts, our skills, and our passions to this great endeavour. We each play our small part but together we have but one purpose – to glorify God and to enjoy Him forever.

6. The body rejoices and suffers together

Lastly, it is important to remember that the organic unity of the body of Christ means that when one part of it suffers, the whole body suffers. Return to the analogy of the physical body for a moment and the issue becomes clear. When you are ill because you have a kidney infection, you do not say that your kidney is ill, do you? You say that you are ill because you have a kidney infection. When you have a migraine you do not tell people your head has a migraine, you say that you have a migraine. The same blood flows throughout the whole body. That means that when one part of your body is not working properly, you are ill, not just that one part of your body. The same is true for the church. If one part rejoices, all parts rejoice. If one part weeps, then all parts weep (Romans 12:15). Martyn Lloyd-Jones, comments on this reality:

> If we truly understood this doctrine of the Church, any idea of competition, rivalry, self-seeking, self-importance would be utterly impossible, indeed it would be ludicrous. And as and when we are guilty of such things we are simply proclaiming that we have never understood the doctrine of the Church.[54]

Every person who has come to faith in God through the new birth is part of the one body of Christ. In the words of Paul to the Galatians:

> But now that faith has come, we are no longer subject to a disciplinarian, for in Christ Jesus you are all children of God through faith. As many of you as were baptized into Christ

have clothed yourselves with Christ. There is no longer Jew or Greek, there is no longer slave or free, there is no longer male and female; for all of you are one in Christ Jesus.

Galatians 3:25–28

What a remarkable privilege to be part of one body. We so often forget these basic truths and allow ourselves to become locked away in isolation from one another. There is such beauty and strength, however, in the body of Christ celebrating its unity and allowing its life to flow across every part of it. That life is a shared life because it is the life of the third Person of the Trinity. He is given to God's people.

It is to the Holy Spirit that we now turn our attention as we continue to reflect on Paul's seven principles of unity in the church.

Reflection

Do you actually know what is going on in the life of the church more widely? Why not think about doing just three simple things. Firstly, find out what is happening in the other local churches in your community and see if your church family can help in any way. Secondly, commit to praying for the national leaders of the church in the United Kingdom. Thirdly, join the mailing list of an organization that is working with the globally persecuted church and make sure that the needs, blessings, and challenges of the worldwide church are highlighted regularly in your congregation.

Are there individual families in your church or your wider community who would benefit from your help and support and care? Perhaps you know someone who is facing tough decisions or a hard time in their family. How can you come alongside them without patronizing them? What can you do to strengthen family life in your own home or the family life of another family you know? How can you share life and share Jesus with another family?

One Spirit – A Shared Life

I f the church is one body then what gives us life? The answer is given to us by the Apostle Paul in the second phrase that he uses in Ephesians 4:4 as he reminds the Ephesian believers that they are united by one Spirit. The Holy Spirit brings life to the church like breath brings life to the natural body. He permeates the entirety of the church and He is undivided. There is only one Holy Spirit. He is an indivisible Person and therefore the life that we have from Him is indivisible. Just as a human body breathes in oxygen and that oxygen is used to sustain every aspect of the body, from the mouth and nostrils at the point of entry all the way down to the fingertips, so the Holy Spirit is the source of life for any part of the church and every member of the body of Christ. It is because He is undivided and indivisible that we are undivided and indivisible.

He is not simply a force, or a power, or an aura. He has a personality and can be grieved (see, for example, Ephesians 4:30); He speaks (for example, Ezekiel 2:2; Matthew 10:19–20; 1 Timothy 4:1–2); He guides (John 16:13; Acts 16:6–11); and He intercedes (Romans 8:26). We do not refer to Him as an object or by using the pronoun "it". The Scriptures always describe Him in personal terms. Jesus speaks of Him very clearly in this way, describing Him repeatedly as the Advocate or the Spirit of truth:

"And I will ask the Father, and he will give you another Advocate, to be with you forever. This is the Spirit of truth, whom the world cannot receive, because it neither sees him nor knows him. You know him, because he abides in you, and he will be with you."

John 14:16–17

"I have said these things to you while I am still with you. But the Advocate, the Holy Spirit, whom the Father will send in my name, will teach you everything, and remind you of all that I have said to you."

John 14:25–26

"When the Advocate comes, whom I will send to you from the Father, the Spirit of truth who comes from the Father, he will testify on my behalf."

John 15:26

"Nevertheless, I tell you the truth: it is to your advantage that I go away, for if I do not go away, the Advocate will not come to you; but if I go, I will send him to you. And when he comes, he will prove the world wrong about sin and righteousness and judgement: about sin, because they do not believe in me; about righteousness, because I am going to the Father and you will see me no longer; about judgement, because the ruler of this world has been condemned.

"I still have many things to say to you, but you cannot bear them now. When the Spirit of truth comes, he will guide you into all the truth; for he will not speak on his own, but will speak whatever he hears, and he will declare to you the things that are to come. He will glorify me, because he will take what

is mine and declare it to you. All that the Father has is mine. For this reason I said that he will take what is mine and declare it to you."

John 16:7–15

How the Spirit unites us

He unites us as our Advocate, our plumb line and our DNA

As a Person and a part of the Trinity, the Holy Spirit consistently remains true to His purposes, and as a result of this consistency in His own ministry there is essential spiritual unity within the church of Jesus Christ. It is clear that He unites us as our Advocate and as the Spirit of truth. He unites us as our Advocate because He defends us before the world when it accuses us and before the devil when he tries to trick us, discourage us, or destroy us. And as our Advocate, He uses the same standard of truth for all of us. There is not one set of truth that can be used for His favourites, because God has no favourites (Romans 2:11). He uses the truth of who God is, what God has said, and what God is seeking to do in the world to guide us, instruct us, protect us, challenge us, and inspire us. That is why it is so important for the church across the United Kingdom to remember that we find our identity in the truths of Scripture and how God has instructed us. The Bible, inspired by God and breathed out by the Holy Spirit (2 Timothy 3:16; 2 Peter 1:21), is the standard of truth, or the plumb line, against which we measure ourselves. The Spirit holds us accountable to the truths of God, not just to the acceptable norms of our culture.

That is not to say that He does not evidence His work and His presence differently in each of our different lives and in each of our different contexts, but the differences are only superficial. We carry the likeness of the Spirit in individual ways. Different family members in the same family are a helpful illustration. No two family members are the same. They are in one family but they have different traits and characteristics. Even identical twins are never exactly the same. Within the one church there are many different individuals with their own characteristics and traits but the same Spirit is at work across and in them all. The one Spirit unites us all. The Holy Spirit is the life of the church and therefore He shares His life across the whole body, and His life is consistent, even when we as local churches or as individual Christians are different (1 Corinthians 12). It is precisely because we are not rolled off a factory production line looking and sounding identical to one another that the manifestation of the Spirit's life and work in us will vary. This in and of itself is a powerful indicator of the unity that God has given to His church through His Spirit. When the Holy Spirit does God's work in us, it is essentially the same work in all Christians, although it might manifest itself differently in each of us. He takes each of us as we are and brings about a family likeness in us (Romans 8:15). We are becoming like the Father (1 John 3:1ff) as we are changed from one degree of glory to another (2 Corinthians 3:18). We share, in the Holy Spirit, a common Advocate, a common plumb line of truth, and a common spiritual DNA. It is through Him that we become like the Father, and as we become like the Father, we inevitably come closer and closer to one another. This is exactly what Christ prayed for us in John 17.

He unites us as He builds and inhabits us as God's temple

At the end of Ephesians 2, Paul reminds the believers in Ephesus of what God is doing in their lives:

> *So then you are no longer strangers and aliens, but you are citizens with the saints and also members of the household of God, built upon the foundation of the apostles and prophets, with Christ Jesus himself as the cornerstone. In him the whole structure is joined together and grows into a holy temple in the Lord; in whom you also are built together spiritually into a dwelling place for God.*
>
> Ephesians 2:19–22

The last phrase of what Paul writes to the Ephesians is better rendered as, "In whom you are also built together in the Spirit into a dwelling place for God."

Paul reminds them, in other words, that God is at work in them by the power of the Holy Spirit, continually enabling them to be a new temple, a collective dwelling place for the presence of God Himself. The image that Paul paints would have been familiar to his readers: the picture of a physical temple being built out of stones. In order to build the temple, the stones would have been quarried and then dressed by stonemasons so that they could fit together properly in the building. Paul tells the believers in Ephesus that this is what the Holy Spirit does in them. The Spirit is the Stonemason who prepares them to be a dwelling place for God. At the same time the Spirit is the one who indwells them individually and collectively because He is the very breath and presence of God.

It is a beautiful picture of the work of the Holy Spirit in the lives of individual believers and in the life of the church collectively. In making us part of the one body that is the church, the Holy Spirit carries out a number of functions that are common to all believers, as well as doing specific work in each of us that is unique to us.

He unites us through conviction and conversion

If we are not careful, we can identity the positive things that the Spirit does in us and ignore the more challenging things that He does in us. That is because some of the work of the Spirit is uncomfortable for us in the short term while it is good for us in the long term, and most of us like to think in the short term only. One of the apparently less comfortable and less obvious things the Holy Spirit does to unite us is convict us of sin and bring us to a point of trust in Christ – what we call conversion.

We cannot become part of the invisible church without the work of the Spirit, but what are the requirements for entry into God's family? It is important that God holds all people to the same standard, and therefore we each need the convicting and converting power of the Holy Spirit to be at work in our lives if we are to become part of the body of Christ. Without the Spirit's work and presence in our lives we are unprepared and unable to be part of that body. The Apostle Paul makes this abundantly clear to the believers in Corinth:

> *Do you not know that wrongdoers will not inherit the kingdom of God? Do not be deceived! Fornicators, idolaters, adulterers, male prostitutes, sodomites, thieves, the greedy,*

drunkards, revilers, robbers – none of these will inherit the kingdom of God. And this is what some of you used to be. But you were washed, you were sanctified, you were justified in the name of the Lord Jesus Christ and in the Spirit of our God.

1 Corinthians 6:9–11

Before anyone can be part of the body of Christ, the church, the Holy Spirit must do His work of conviction. The idea of conviction is largely perceived as a negative one today because of the associations with a court of law, but within the context of Christian faith it is not a negative concept at all. The idea of being confronted with our shortcomings and our failings is not something any of us are particularly comfortable with. If we remember that it is through an acknowledgment of our own weaknesses and by recognizing our dependence upon God that we are brought into His family, then our understanding of conviction changes. Couple that with the principle that all people share the frailty and shortcoming of sin and that none of us deserves to be part of Christ's body, and the unifying power of the Holy Spirit's conviction is understood even more clearly because we are able to see that there is hope for all of us. Recall the words of Jesus to His disciples in the Farewell Discourse that I quoted earlier:

"Nevertheless, I tell you the truth: it is to your advantage that I go away, for if I do not go away, the Advocate will not come to you; but if I go, I will send Him to you. And when he comes, he will prove the world wrong about sin and righteousness and judgement: about sin, because they do not believe in me; about righteousness, because I am going to the Father and you will see me no longer; about judgement, because the ruler of this world has been condemned.

"I still have many things to say to you, but you cannot bear them now. When the Spirit of truth comes, he will guide you into all the truth; for he will not speak on his own, but will speak whatever he hears, and he will declare to you the things that are to come. He will glorify me, because he will take what is mine and declare it to you. All that the Father has is mine. For this reason I said that he will take what is mine and declare it to you."

John 16:7–15

The Holy Spirit confronts us with our own failings and inadequacies and our need of a Saviour. He exposes the brokenness of our lives and the failures of our hearts. It is the work of the Spirit in all believers that takes us from a place of not realizing we need a Saviour to realizing that we do. Whether He uses the rites and rituals of the visible church that we have been part of to do this or He confronts us through a deepening awareness of our own shortcomings and failings is entirely up to Him. Some Christians are brought to saving faith through their lifelong participation in the life of a local church. Others reach the place of personal conviction without ever having set foot in a church. The method does not matter because it is the principle that is important.

A friend of mine grew up within the Anglican Church. He was baptized as a baby and confirmed as a young man. In between those two important moments of confession in his life something powerful happened. His baptism was a step of covenant and anticipation taken by his parents, and his confirmation was his own choice to affirm the promises made over him as a child and to stand upon them in his own right. In between those two moments in his life he attended church, was brought up with the Creed, and was taught the tenets of the Christian faith. Over his years of church attendance the Holy Spirit used what he was hearing week by week as well as the lives of other Christians around him to help him see that there was an enormous difference between being churched and being converted. He never experienced a single moment of conversion. He cannot point back to a certain date and time in his life when he invited Christ to take control of his destiny and he sought the forgiveness of his sins for the first time. The Holy Spirit drew him into faith slowly, gently, and through a whole childhood and adolescence of godly influences and voices. He is aware, however, that he has crossed from a place of ascribing to other people's beliefs to having a personal faith in God. He is aware of his constant need of the saving power of Christ and the forgiveness of God that was obtained for him at the cross. He is aware of his own brokenness and sinfulness, and over time he has turned in repentance to the Lord for new life and new hope. All of this is a result of the convicting power of the Holy Spirit.

My story is very different. I was not brought up in a churchgoing family. We were Presbyterians by birth but not by practice. I was christened as a child but that christening was never explained to me. I was not schooled in the ways of God or the truths of the Christian faith. The way in which the Holy Spirit convicted me was not at all like my Anglican friend's journey to faith. I can remember attending a children's holiday club as a six- or seven-year-old boy. It was held in a small local Pentecostal church on the Doagh Road in Newtownabbey. During the summer holidays each year a team from the church would visit the local estate where I lived and do detached children's work. They invited us to come along and take part in a week of special activities. We would sing songs, play games, and win prizes. We would also get a drink and a snack. If you are a six- or seven-year-old boy, bored with nothing to do in the summer holidays, what is not to love about the chance to have a bit of fun? So I went along. I can remember the leaders talking about a God who loved us and knew us inside out. They said that even though we did wrong things God still loved us and wanted to be our friend. They explained that God's Son, Jesus, had died for us and that if we said sorry to Him then He would wash away our guilt and welcome us into His family. I know this was a very basic presentation of the gospel message but I can still remember now, as a middle-aged man, feeling its power in my life. I responded to the invitation to ask Jesus to be my friend, and I can still remember the feeling of lightness and joy that I felt immediately when I prayed with one of the leaders. I believe that was the first time I sensed the conviction of the Holy Spirit and the consequent freedom that forgiveness and hope could truly bring. It may have been my conversion, but I am not sure. I think about it often.

My attendance at church did not last more than a few weeks. With no children's club to go to and no one to take me to the meetings I quickly turned my attention to other things. Yet throughout the next three or four years of my primary school education and into my secondary school, as I approached being a teenager, I remembered that single week of my childhood. I joined the Boys' Brigade and went to a local church every Sunday as part of my commitment to the Brigade. Again I was asked if I would commit my life to Jesus and again I said yes because I sensed a deep conviction of my wrongdoing and my sinfulness. My friend in primary school, Paul McConaghie, took me along to the church, and it lasted for a few years, but again it trailed off. One again the Holy Spirit was working in me, convicting me. He was showing me that there was something not right at the centre of my life and that it needed to be addressed.

I had an elderly great-aunt who was a deeply committed Christian. My Aunt Maureen and Uncle Gilbert were faithful attendees of a famous church called Whitewell in north Belfast. One summer I spent a few weeks with them and they took me to church with them. I must have been about eleven or twelve. Once again I made a commitment to Christ, but it did not last. When I went home my commitment faded away.

In secondary school I had a friend called Graham Clark. He was also a committed Christian and I saw something in him that I really wanted. His mum had died and he had coped with it amazingly well. I can remember sensing, again, that God was challenging me. When I was sixteen years of age Graham invited me to an open-air meeting in Belfast. I went along one Friday afternoon and listened to the preacher, and as I did I heard an audible voice. It felt like someone was standing behind me and whispering in my ear, "Son, come home." It was so real that I turned to see who was speaking to me, but there was no one there. I knew it was the voice of God. Do not ask me how I knew, but I just knew.

That weekend I went to the church that my aunt and uncle attended and I listened to the preacher. He did not know me at all as the church was so large and there was no way he could have remembered me from my brief visit four or five years before. As I was leaving, he called out to me across the foyer of the church and said, "Son, come home." He used precisely the same words I had heard on the Friday afternoon! At that moment, as a sixteen-year-old boy who was becoming a man, I finally surrendered my life fully to Christ. That was the moment I was converted, I think. Some would argue that I was actually converted as a six- or seven-year-old boy. I might have been, but I think that what began when I was six or seven resulted in my full and final decision to follow Christ when I was sixteen.

My story of conviction is very different from my friend's, but we were both convicted by the same Holy Spirit. We were both confronted with our sin. We were both challenged to surrender our lives to Jesus. That is because the one Holy Spirit was doing the same work in both of our lives in different ways. Whatever way He does it, the Holy Spirit does a work of conviction in the lives of all Christians to draw them into the family of God. He meets some dramatically, like He did with me. He meets others gently, like He did with my friend. Others are drawn to the point of conviction not by seeing how broken they are necessarily but by seeing the vastness and the utter beauty of God. The Holy Spirit can use music, creation, conversation, Scripture, friends, trials, moments of success or failure, joys, sorrows, or probing and unsettling questions to draw us to the point where we become aware that we need a Saviour. The way He does it is up to Him. The fact that He does it with all believers means that we are brought to the point of entrance to the same family of God by the same Spirit.

This work of conviction does not end with our conversion. It continues throughout our Christian lives. The Holy Spirit continues to draw our attention to those areas of our attitudes and behaviours that are incongruent with the holiness of God and His purposes for our lives as outlined in Scripture. The same Spirit uses the same truth to lead us to the same Father.

He unites us through His gift of life – both individually and as part of the church

The Holy Spirit also brings new life to all believers. Without His life, we have no real spiritual life. One aspect of this is what some refer to as the work of regeneration, while others might describe it as quickening.[55] Put simply, genuine Christian faith is impossible without the life of the Spirit bringing it to birth. Jesus Himself made this abundantly clear to the religious leader, Nicodemus:

> *"Very truly, I tell you, no one can enter the kingdom of God without being born of water and Spirit. What is born of the flesh is flesh, and what is born of the Spirit is spirit. Do not be astonished that I said to you, 'You must be born from above.' The wind blows where it chooses, and you hear the sound of it, but you do not know where it comes from or where it goes. So it is with everyone who is born of the Spirit."*
>
> John 3:5–8

In addition, no continued Christian life is possible without the Holy Spirit being constantly present. It is only by the work of the one Spirit that we are enabled to be part of the one body. Without this powerful work of the Spirit we cannot be part of the body, and without this powerful work of the Spirit in each of us there can be no unity in the one body, the church. Paul emphasizes this reality to the believers in Rome:

But you are not in the flesh; you are in the Spirit, since the Spirit of God dwells in you. Anyone who does not have the Spirit of Christ does not belong to him.

Romans 8:9

Having established so clearly the centrality of the presence and work of the Holy Spirit in the lives of all believers, Paul goes on to explain that the very life of the Spirit becomes the life of all believers. The Spirit not only brings life into us, He also brings us into the life of God and into the family of the church:

But if Christ is in you, though the body is dead because of sin, the Spirit is life because of righteousness. If the Spirit of him who raised Jesus from the dead dwells in you, he who raised Christ from the dead will give life to your mortal bodies also through his Spirit that dwells in you.

Romans 8:10–11

He goes on to argue that it is the life and presence of the Holy Spirit in the believer that gives us the assurance that we are indeed part of God's family:

For you did not receive a spirit of slavery to fall back into fear, but you have received a spirit of adoption. When we cry, "Abba! Father!" it is that very Spirit bearing witness with our spirit that we are children of God, and if children, then heirs, heirs of God and joint heirs with Christ – if, in fact, we suffer with him so that we may also be glorified with him.

Romans 8:15–17

Paul roots the presence of the life of the Spirit in the lives of believers in the promises of God to the people of Israel. These promises were that God would place His Spirit in His people and that He would dwell with them and in them. In Paul's second letter to the believers in Corinth, he reminds them of the promises found in Leviticus 26:12 and Exodus 29:45:

> For we are the temple of the living God; as God said,
>> "I will live in them and walk among them,
>> and I will be their God,
>> and they shall be my people."
>
> 2 Corinthians 6:16

Believers in the early church had a clear understanding that their life in God was dependent upon God's life in them. It was inconceivable to the early church that they could exist as believers or as a community of believers without the presence and the power of the Spirit's life within them. They were deeply rooted in the reality of His power and presence from the very beginning.

As we read the story of the first few decades of the church's life, we are brought again and again to the realization that they were utterly dependent upon the Spirit's life. This reality prevents any view of the church as a mere organization, because the presence of the Spirit forms the church and is the basis of its unity.[56] From Luke's opening remarks in Acts that Jesus was giving them commands through the Spirit's power (Acts 1:2), all the way to the last phrase of the same book which describes Paul as preaching and teaching about Jesus Christ boldly and bravely in Rome without hindrance (Acts 28:31), the story of the early church could be described as the story of the power, presence, and purpose of the Holy Spirit. They were told to wait for the presence of the Spirit (Acts 1:4, 8); they were promised an immersion into the power of the Holy Spirit (Acts 1:5); their whole purpose was shaped by the words of Scripture, spoken by the Holy Spirit (Acts 1:16). They had been birthed by the pouring out of the Holy Spirit on the day of Pentecost (Acts 2:1–4). When Peter stood to explain what was happening on that day, he used the words of the prophet Joel to help the onlookers understand what was happening (Acts 2:16–21; Joel 2:28–32). Not only that, but as the crowd listened to Peter, they responded by asking him what they must do in response to his declaration about the purposes of God in Christ. His response is clear:

> *"Repent, and be baptized every one of you in the name of Jesus Christ so that your sins may be forgiven; and you will receive the gift of the Holy Spirit. For the promise is for you, for your children, and for all who are far away, everyone whom the Lord our God calls to him."*
>
> Acts 2:38–39

It was the Spirit's life and power that they shared with others. After all, they had little else they could give to those around them (Acts 3:6). Peter addressed rulers and leaders in the power of the Spirit (Acts 4:8). As they tried to work out who they were and what their place in the world was, with persecution and uncertainty all around them, it was the Spirit's power that renewed them and gave them courage (Acts 4:31). The Spirit kept them from deceit and exposed deception among them (Acts 5:1–11). The Spirit was within them and alongside them, guiding them and protecting them (Acts 5:32). When the Jerusalem church faced a crisis because of potential division, the leaders sought to find people who evidenced the Spirit's power and presence to become a new band of servant leaders (Acts 6:3). The Spirit's power inspired and anointed Stephen, the first Christian martyr (Acts 7:51, 55). It was the Spirit who gave the believers their distinctiveness in Samaria (Acts 8:15, 17–19). He guided them as individuals in situations such as Philip being led to the Ethiopian charioteer (Acts 8:29ff), Barnabas and Saul being set aside for ministry (Acts 13:1–2), and when the early church met in Jerusalem (Acts 15). The Apostle Paul was filled with the Spirit shortly after his conversion (Acts 9:17), and the church grew and multiplied by the power of the Spirit (Acts 9:31). They were led into new territory by the Spirit (Acts 10:19), and the Spirit's life was given to those who entered the church from a Gentile background (Acts 10:38, 44–45, 47). In his report back to the Jerusalem church, Peter explains his actions with the Gentiles as a direct response to the leading of the Holy Spirit (Acts 11:12, 15–16). The list could go on and on. Indeed, the Spirit is explicitly mentioned in the book of Acts at least sixty-four times.

This common gift of the Spirit's life to all of the people of God remains central to our self-understanding and our understanding of one another. We cannot be found in Christ without also being found in His body, the church. The Spirit is one of the great sources of life to the people of God both individually and collectively. It is through the Spirit that each of us and all of us are enabled to be partakers of the divine nature of God (2 Peter 1:4). We share His life in His body. Paul reminds the Corinthians of this:

*For in the one Spirit we were all baptized into one body –
Jews or Greeks, slaves or free – and we were all made to drink
of one Spirit.*

1 Corinthians 12:13

This is not the theological property of one branch of the church and cannot be confined to a charismatic or Pentecostal perspective. The life of the Spirit is biblically central to all believers everywhere. Without the Spirit of God in our lives, we cannot function as Christians or as the church. For that reason, when we allow other secondary ways in which we define ourselves, such as denominational affiliation, language, culture, custom, or nationality, to become more important than the vital and unifying work of the Holy Spirit, then we will become divided. It is only as we allow the Spirit and His life to be the primary force in us and the primary shaper of us that we are able to maintain the unity of the church. Perhaps that is why Paul says what he does in the verses immediately prior to his great sevenfold declaration of unity:

*… making every effort to maintain the unity of the Spirit in
the bond of peace.*

Ephesians 4:3

It is challenging to think that most of the divisions in the church of Jesus Christ are caused because we have failed to recognize the primacy of the work of the Holy Spirit in one another and the bond that He creates between us. This is particularly true when we realize that one of the New Testament litmus tests for the genuineness of our faith is whether or not we love others in Christ's church. John reminds his readers:

For this is the message that you have heard from the beginning, that we should love one another. We must not be like Cain who was from the evil one and murdered his brother. And why did he murder him? Because his own deeds were evil and his brother's righteous. Do not be astonished, brothers and sisters, that the world hates you. We know that we have passed from death to life because we love one another. Whoever does not love abides in death. All who hate a brother or sister are murderers, and you know that murderers do not have eternal life abiding in them. We know love by this, that he laid down his life for us – and we ought to lay down our lives for one another. How does God's love abide in anyone who has the world's goods and sees a brother or sister in need and yet refuses help?

1 John 3:11–17

We share His life with every moment of our existence as believers, yet we sometimes fail to see His life in one another. There can be no life and there can be no unity in the church without the work of the Holy Spirit because there can be no church where the Holy Spirit is not at work. Commenting on the reality of the Spirit's work in all believers throughout the Church, John Stott writes:

First, there is one body because there is only one Spirit (verse 4).[57] The one body is the church, the body of Christ (1:23), comprising Jewish and Gentile believers; and its unity and cohesion is due to the one Holy Spirit who indwells and animates it. As Paul writes elsewhere, "By one Spirit we were all baptised into one body – Jews or Greeks, slaves or free – and all were made to drink of one Spirit."[58] Thus it is our common possession of the one Holy Spirit that integrates us into one body.[59]

He unites us through common fruit

When the Spirit is present and at work in our lives there are tell-tale signs that are visible to others as well as to us. He may be an invisible presence, but the effects of His presence are demonstrable. Just as the wind is not visible but its effects can be seen, so the Spirit may be invisible but there are clear indicators of Him at work in a Christian and in a church.

The Holy Spirit produces fruit in the lives of Christians everywhere. Paul lists some of that fruit, though surely not all, in his letter to the Galatians:

> *But the fruit of the [Holy] Spirit [the work which His presence within accomplishes] is love, joy (gladness), peace, patience (an even temper, forbearance), kindness, goodness (benevolence), faithfulness, gentleness (meekness, humility), self-control (self-restraint, continence). Against such things there is no law [that can bring a charge]. And those who belong to Christ Jesus (the Messiah) have crucified the flesh (the godless human nature) with its passions and appetites and desires. If we live by the [Holy] Spirit, let us also walk by the Spirit. [If by the Holy Spirit we have our life in God, let us go forward walking in line, our conduct controlled by the Spirit.]*

> Galatians 5:22–25 (AMP)

Imagine for a moment what it would look and feel like to be part of a church where all of these traits were visible in all of the people. Take the characteristic of love as an example. What would a church look like where there was a heartfelt sense of love for one another, genuine and evidenced in the way we spoke of and responded to one another? Imagine if that love was as enduring, trusting, believing, tangible, and beautiful as the love that is described by the Apostle Paul in his letter to the Corinthians (1 Corinthians 13). What would that feel like?

Now work your way down the list of the nine fruit of the Spirit that Paul mentions in Galatians 5. I cannot imagine that a church that exhibited these characteristics would ever be divided. Challenges would be talked through. The best would be believed of one another. Resentments would be addressed. Such a church would make room for differences of personality and approach. Ungodly behaviour would be named and addressed in an atmosphere of grace and truth. I think I would walk across hot coals to be part of a church family like that! It is one thing to believe that these characteristics are a common work of the Holy Spirit, but it is quite another to actually allow Him to produce these traits in us. The truth is that all of our theology must eventually become biography if the world is to take our faith seriously.[60]

It is often said that no church is perfect because there is no such thing as a perfect person. That is most definitely true. We let one another down. We argue. We fail to see another person's point of view. We are too hot-headed. We often fail to acknowledge that we might be wrong. On more than one occasion I have said to a congregation that if they want to be part of a perfect church they should be careful not to ask me to join it because I am far from perfect. I am flawed and broken and I do not always allow the Holy Spirit to control my temperament. None of that, however, should be seen as an excuse for patterns of behaviour in my life as a Christian and as a leader of Christ's church that allows me to dodge the challenge of letting the fruit of the Spirit be developed and evidenced in my life. My overarching desire as a follower of Jesus is to allow the fruit of the Spirit to become increasingly evidenced in my actions and my responses and to see my temperament increasingly controlled by the Spirit. I fail in this area so often. Like the Apostle Paul, I sometimes feel that:

> *I do not understand my own actions. For I do not do what I want, but I do the very thing I hate… For I do not do the good I want, but the evil I do not want to do is what I do.*
>
> Romans 7:15, 19

I can explain away my weaknesses and poor choices because of my background, my genetics, and my natural temperament, yet I am challenged by the words of Dr Henry Brandt:

> *You can use your background as an excuse for present behaviour only until you receive Jesus Christ as your personal Lord and Saviour. After that, you have a new power within you that is able to change your conduct.*[61]

The Spirit's presence in the lives of all Christians and His common work in producing His character traits in us is supposed to be more than a theological conviction that we hold. It is also supposed to be the source of the transformation of our personal character. A common commitment to love, joy, peace, patience, kindness, generosity, faithfulness, gentleness, and self-control would utterly transform the lives of local churches and the relationship between churches in a town or a city. It would also utterly transform the relationships within families.

The absence of the fruit of the Spirit in the lives of Christians doesn't only affect churches and congregations. It can be seen in the heartbreak of families that have lost one another too. As a pastor, I have spent hundreds of hours with family conflict. I have walked the sad and painful road of separation and divorce with many. I have tried to help parents connect with estranged children. I have seen the gut-wrenching impact of grandparents being separated from their grandchildren. There are often very complex reasons why families break down. As a pastor, I want to help them stay together as best I can and help them to address the issues that caused the chasms to open up in their relationships in the first place.

The pain and devastation of family disintegration can be catastrophic. Yet in every single situation where I have witnessed this kind of trauma, it would have been drastically altered if the fruit of the Spirit had been in evidence somehow. One person finds it hard to forgive another. A husband loses patience with his wife. A wife falls out of love with her husband. A teenager develops an attitude of entitlement instead of gratitude. An absence of generosity means that the family no longer speaks well of one another and words of affirmation are lost. Kindness is replaced with cruelty. Patience is eaten up by pettiness. Love is dissolved by complacency and familiarity. In the end, it doesn't matter whether the community that is divided is a business, a church, or a family. The absence of the common traits of the fruit of the Spirit will eventually lead to disaster, disintegration, and separation.

It is legitimate, even if it is difficult, to ask whether God is genuinely at work in someone's life when that person fails to exhibit any change in their character over time. It is very possible for an individual to have an intellectual understanding of the gospel and the work of Christ without that understanding ever resulting in their personal transformation. An absence of the fruit of the Spirit warrants a question about the validity of an individual's experience of Christ.

What is true of individuals is also true of church. A whole community can convince themselves that they are a Christian community because they have attested to certain intellectual beliefs. Those beliefs, however, have a transformative power in the life of the community when they are truly held and not just intellectually affirmed. Our theology must eventually become biography.

John Calvin's approach to Ephesians 4:4 suggests that the phrase we are considering, "there is one body and one Spirit", would be better translated as "there is one body and one soul".[62] I am not sure that is the right approach to the words, given the wider context of Paul's meaning in the passage, but I am struck by the way Calvin challenges his reader to think about the implications of God's work in the lives of all believers:

> *Oh, were this thought deeply impressed upon our minds, that we are subject to a law which no more permits the children of God to differ among themselves than the kingdom of heaven to be divided, how earnestly should we cultivate brotherly kindness! How should we dread every kind of animosity, if we duly reflected that all who separate us from the brethren, estrange us from the kingdom of God! And yet, strangely enough, while we forget the duties which brethren owe to each other, we go on boasting that we are the sons of God. Let us learn from Paul that none are at all fit for that inheritance who are not one body and one spirit.*[63]

A public confession of faith in Christ that is not accompanied by a commitment to love one another is a contradiction in terms. No wonder the world around us is sometimes confused about the church.

He unites us through shared gifts

A further evidence of the Spirit's life in all of the church is the way in which He gives gifts and abilities to those who are part of the body of Christ. Different denominations and streams have differing views on which of these gifts remain available to the church. Cessationists believe that some of the gifts of the Spirit, such as speaking in tongues, prophecy, and healing, ceased with the death of the last original apostle. They would also argue, therefore, that the gifts of apostles and prophets are no longer to be understood in the ways in which the New Testament describes them. Cessationists would, however, continue to hold that many of the gifts of the New Testament era continue to be given to people by the Holy Spirit. They would see the gifts of pastors, teachers, and evangelists, for example, as still very much part of the church's life and witness. Other Christians believe that all the gifts of the Spirit remain available to Christians today. Personally, I would describe myself as sitting in the latter camp, as I believe that every gift evidenced in the New Testament is available for the church today and that the Holy Spirit gives these gifts to Christians so that the purposes of God can be accomplished.

There are a number of lists in the New Testament that outline the gifts that the Holy Spirit brings to believers. Passages such as 1 Corinthians 12:8–11, Ephesians 4:7–13, and Romans 12:3–8 outline some of these gifts. They are illustrative lists rather than exhaustive, and demonstrate ways in which the Holy Spirit enabled the early church to accomplish the purposes of God. Today, the same Spirit continues to give gifts to the church to enable the people of God to fulfil the purposes of God on the earth.

> *To one is given through the Spirit the utterance of wisdom, and to another the utterance of knowledge according to the same Spirit, to another faith by the same Spirit, to another gifts of healing by the one Spirit, to another the working of miracles, to another prophecy, to another the discernment of spirits, to another various kinds of tongues, to another the interpretation of tongues. All these are activated by one and the same Spirit, who allots to each one individually just as the Spirit chooses.*
>
> 1 Corinthians 12:8–11

> *But each of us was given grace according to the measure of Christ's gift. Therefore it is said, "When he ascended on high he made captivity itself a captive; he gave gifts to his people."*
>
> *(When it says, "He ascended", what does it mean but that he had also descended into the lower parts of the earth? He who descended is the same one who ascended far above all the heavens, so that he might fill all things.) The gifts he gave were that some would be apostles, some prophets, some evangelists, some pastors and teachers, to equip the saints for the work of ministry, for building up the body of Christ, until all of us come to the unity of the faith and of the knowledge of the Son of God, to maturity, to the measure of the full stature of Christ.*
>
> Ephesians 4:7–13

> *For by the grace given to me I say to everyone among you not to think of yourself more highly than you ought to think, but to*

think with sober judgement, each according to the measure of faith that God has assigned. For as in one body we have many members, and not all the members have the same function, so we, who are many, are one body in Christ, and individually we are members one of another. We have gifts that differ according to the grace given to us: prophecy, in proportion to faith; ministry, in ministering; the teacher, in teaching; the exhorter, in exhortation; the giver, in generosity; the leader, in diligence; the compassionate, in cheerfulness.

Romans 12:3–8

I am trying to set out which gifts are valid today and which are no longer available. The point I am seeking to make is that in the same way as the Holy Spirit brings fruit into the lives of all Christians, He gives gifts to God's people. In the giving of fruit He enables us to love one another and to live as a community united by a common commitment to the same values, virtues, and behaviours. In the giving of His gifts, He enables us to work alongside one another as the church. It seems to me to matter very little whether you describe a church leader as a pastor, a vicar, a minister, or a priest. The important thing is that the leader of the local church is endowed with gifts by the Holy Spirit so that she or he can lead the church well. Some churches are governed and led by elders, others by deacons. Some, such as the Anglican Church and the Roman Catholic Church, have an Episcopalian approach to leadership which means that they have archbishops, bishops, priests, and so forth who work with churchwardens and the parochial church council to bring leadership to the congregation. Others, such as the Presbyterian Church of Ireland or the Elim Pentecostal Church, have a structure which encourages pastors or ministers to work with elders and church sessions in the leadership of the congregation. The Baptists very often work with ministers and deacons (who form a diaconate) to lead the local community of faith.

Behind this plethora of titles and roles, however, sit the gifts of the Holy Spirit as given to individuals in local churches to enable them to function well and to further the kingdom of God. All the gifts are given for the common good, the common purpose being the building up of the body of Christ (Ephesians 4:12). "To each is given the manifestation of the Spirit for the common good" (1 Corinthians 12:7).

In the words of Geoffrey Wainwright, "The diverse gifts and functions in the Church are all, according to the Apostle Paul, contained in the one body, in whose service they stand."[64]

The church's common purpose is served by the Spirit's gifts across the body of Christ. Just as not every local church will have every single gift of the Spirit, so I would suggest that not every denomination has every single gift of the Spirit. In fact, I wonder whether God has deliberately given specific gifts and passions to different streams in order to remind the whole body of Christ that we need one another. I am not sure we are terribly good at celebrating the gifts of God's Spirit across the church. We often want to have all the gifts in our own congregation or denomination because we do not want to have to acknowledge our own weaknesses or be forced to look beyond the confines of our own narrow theological worldview to find others with whom God is working.

Toward the end of his book, *Dirty Glory*, Pete Greig, whom God used to found the global 24–7 prayer movement, writes about his yearning for unity:

We are different in culture, geography, psychology, and even theology, of course, but that's what makes it fun! Surely we could learn to look at each other generously and, instead of wondering, "What's wrong with them?" we could ask, "What's right with them? What can I learn from them? How can I season my current convictions with a little more humility?"

Of course no one admits to "hating" his Christian brother or sister outright. But in my own life I admit that I have sometimes been competitive and judgmental towards other parts of God's family. I have secretly resented the success of others and been critical of viewpoints I haven't taken the time to comprehend. It's easy to do. On one occasion I was reading a newspaper report about a terrible child abuse scandal in a particular denomination and realised that my gut feeling had been relief that it was "them and not us." Yet in Christ there can only ever be "us." It's disturbingly easy to disguise a critical spirit. To criticise megachurches for consumerism, small churches for lethargy, Pentecostal churches for dualism, traditional churches for dead religion, prosperity churches for exploiting the poor, Reformed churches for reductionism, inclusive churches for syncretism, conservative churches for bigotry. With each new prejudice, we diminish the body of Christ a little more into our own flawed likeness. You can't change the church until you truly love her, and true love accepts imperfections, it forgives hurts, it isn't conditional upon perfection.[65]

The Archbishop of Canterbury and Pope Francis

I long for the day when local congregations share their gifts and their skills more readily and are more open to one another.

On a national and international level, I long for the day when the remarkable gifts and skills that God has placed in other denominations are celebrated by all denominations. Surely the wider church in the United Kingdom can see, and thank God for, the remarkable gift that Justin Welby, the Archbishop of Canterbury, has been to the church in general. Since taking up his post in February 2013 he has been used by God as a significant voice for mission, prayer, and unity. On 21 January 2016 he posted a blog in which he reflected on the challenging journey of the Anglican Church over issues of human sexuality. He wrote of the desire of the Bishops of the Church of England to find a way of walking together, if at all possible. He then reflected on the fragility of the unity in the Anglican Church and commented:

> But that unity is also joyful and astonishing, renewing and nourishing – because it is unity in love for Jesus Christ, whose single family we are, often argumentative, sometimes cruel (which is deeply wrong) but created by God and belonging to each other irrevocably.[66]

In the same way, Pope Francis, who became the leader of the Roman Catholic Church in the same month as Welby became the Archbishop of Canterbury, is surely a gift to the wider body of Christ? His desire and commitment to finding new ways of working with other Christians while acknowledging the theological differences between the Roman Catholic Church and the wider body of Christ has been seen in various initiatives, from discussions with the Orthodox Church and explorations with Pentecostals and Charismatics to the obvious warmth and common purpose he shares with the Archbishop of Canterbury.

During his first week of Prayer for Christian Unity in January 2014, Pope Francis spoke of a clear commitment to walking the path of unity with other Christian leaders:

> *"Unity will not come about as a miracle at the very end,"* he said. *"Rather unity comes about in journeying."*
>
> *"If we do not walk together, if we do not pray for one another, if we do not collaborate in the many ways that we can in this world for the people of God… then unity will not come about."*
>
> *Dialogue and collaboration are essential, he said, but unity will not be the result of human effort, "but rather of the Holy Spirit, who sees our good will".*[67]

We are too ready to dismiss another leader or their gifts to the body of Christ because we disagree with the denomination they are from or their wider theological perspective. A few years ago I was preaching in a country where there was a very sharp divide between Roman Catholicism and Protestantism. I quoted a portion of text from Pope Benedict XVI's book *Jesus of Nazareth*. I consider his books on Jesus to be two of the best I have ever read. There were warm nods from members of the audience as I read the quote, but when I informed the people that it was written by Pope Benedict XVI, not only did the nods become vigorous shakes of the head in disagreement, but also a number of people left the auditorium in protest. Nothing had changed about the words. Nothing had changed about their truthfulness. The only thing that could have caused the reaction was that those who were unhappy could not accept anything written by a pope. How can that be right? I am reminded of the words of the Apostle Paul to the Philippians:

Some proclaim Christ from envy and rivalry, but others from goodwill. These proclaim Christ out of love, knowing that I have been put here for the defence of the gospel; the others proclaim Christ out of selfish ambition, not sincerely but intending to increase my suffering in my imprisonment. What does it matter? Just this, that Christ is proclaimed in every way, whether out of false motives or true; and in that I rejoice.

Philippians 1:15–18

I am not suggesting that we should forget about theological differences between denominations or disregard cherished convictions or beliefs. I am not inferring that those of us outside of the Anglican Church or the Roman Catholic Church should endorse and approve every aspect of their respective theological convictions. Indeed, I would want to investigate and discuss some of those views robustly. But surely the time has come to have a greater openness to the gifts and talents that the Holy Spirit has placed in other parts of Christ's family for the wider benefit of the body of Christ and for the furtherance of the gospel?

He unites us in mission, in worship, and in prayer

The Holy Spirit brings growth to all of the people of God and calls us to proclaim Christ to the ends of the earth (Acts 1:4, 8). He is the Presence that Jesus promised His disciples when Christ gave them the Great Commission (Matthew 28:16–20). He leads us in the mission of God, to live out the Lordship of Christ, and to proclaim the truth of who Jesus is and what Jesus has done. He also gives us an awareness of our intimacy with God the Father (Romans 8:15; Galatians 4:6) and leads us in worship of God

(John 4:24). Indeed, without Him we would be fearful of God and hesitant about standing before our Creator. But the Spirit makes real for us what Jesus has done for us, and enables us to come boldly before Almighty God (Hebrews 4:16).

Our choice of music may vary, our preferences in prayer may be different, and our approaches to sharing the good news of who Jesus Christ is and what He has done may be vastly different across our streams, but if we allow Him to, the Holy Spirit will take our individual contributions and weave them into a beautiful tapestry of ministry in the body of Christ and witness to the world, which will be both challenging and attractive to the world. It is vital to remember that just as the Spirit's fruit is for the whole church and His gifts are for the whole church, so His overarching purposes are for the whole church. If we lose the centrality of His purposes, we lose our souls.

Letting Him unite us by being led by Him

The explosive growth of Pentecostalism over the last century, coupled with the renewal of traditional denominations and the emergence of many new church traditions, has meant that the personality, purposes, and presence of the Holy Spirit have become, perhaps, the most addressed topic in modern theology. Yet all the discussion in the world of who He is and what His purposes are do not translate into an embracing of His ministry in the church. We can discuss Him a great deal but not really make room for Him. I am struck by the challenge of something that I was told A. W. Tozer had once said. I cannot verify it to be true, and have searched in vain to find the original source of the quote. However, I recall hearing a preacher comment that Tozer once said:

If the Holy Spirit was withdrawn from the church today, 95 percent of what we do would go on and no one would know the difference. If the Holy Spirit had been withdrawn from the New Testament church, 95 percent of what they did would stop, and everybody would know the difference.[68]

I wonder how much of what we do and who we are as Christians and as churches is genuinely formed and rooted in the Spirit's personality, purposes, and presence. What is certainly true is that we are called to pay Him more than lip service.

The church is the result of the activity of the Holy Spirit Himself. He was active in the birth of the church at the day of Pentecost (Acts 2). He maintains the church through His work and ministry and presence. He guides the church and continually gives life to her and to all her members.

In his magisterial work on the Holy Spirit, *God's Empowering Presence*, Gordon Fee examines every mention of the Spirit in the teaching of the Apostle Paul. As he pulls his conclusions together, he asks whether many churches have retained a doctrine of the Holy Spirit but lost a sense of His presence and power. He reflects on areas where the church has organized the Spirit onto the sidelines of our communities and then ponders what could be:

I, for one, not only recognise that the clock cannot be turned back, but also find cause for much rejoicing in the church's history. The creeds, the liturgies, the theologizing, the institutional life are not only with us, but for many, myself included, are seen to be the work of the Spirit in the subsequent life of the church. The plea of this study, therefore, is not that of a restorationist, as if we really could restore "the primitive church," whatever that means and whatever that would look like. Rather, it is a plea for the recapturing of the Pauline perspective of Christian life as essentially the life of the Spirit, dynamically experienced and eschatalogically oriented – but fully integrated into the life of the church.

Too much water has passed under the bridge for us to believe that somehow we will be miraculously made one in terms of visible structures, liturgies, and theologies. But time and again, when the human factor is not getting in the way, the Spirit has given God's people a greater sense that they are one across confessional lines. The church is with us – indeed, we are it – in its present shape(s) and structures. May the Spirit of the living God be poured upon it afresh for its life in the present world until Christ comes again.[69]

Reflection

The same Spirit lives in all Christians. How can you allow room for the Holy Spirit in your own life and in the life of your community? Think about the family traits of the Holy Spirit – love, joy, peace, patience, kindness, generosity, faithfulness, gentleness, and self-control – and ask yourself which of these evidences of the Spirit's presence in your life you can see and which you cannot see. Ask God to strengthen the ones that you can see and to grow the ones that you cannot yet see. Begin to use these traits in your life when you speak of others or engage with other people.

Ask God to show you the evidences of the life of His Spirit in the other Christians you meet. At work, ask Him to help you to be a source of these characteristics and to use them in you to bless your workplace. Take some time to ask God to keep you open to the

Spirit's life in your own experience, the experience of your church, and in the experience of the wider church in your community. The churches in your area may not be able to share organizational unity, but how can you enjoy life together? Could you have a shared meal at Christmas or at Pentecost? Perhaps you could combine for an outreach event together? Maybe you could have a joint approach to training or hosting a celebration? What are the things that you can do together to impact your community?

One Hope, One Lord, One Faith, One Baptism – A Shared Future

In 2005 the Labour MP John Spellar, a junior minister in the Northern Ireland office, launched a document called "A Shared Future"[70] in the Province. The document presented the people of Northern Ireland with an encouragement but also with a stark warning. The future of Northern Ireland could be bright or it could be troubled. The people of the Province might decide to live in an unspoken separation, where their children were still segregated in education, their communities still divided on religious and political lines, and their outlooks still coloured by sectarianism and mistrust. Alternatively, they could decide to find ways of reconciling, moving away from mistrust to trust. They could give up fear and find ways to discover one another. The choice was theirs. What was inevitable, however, was the reality that Northern Ireland would be shared. Both sides of the community were going to remain on the island and therefore they needed to make decisions not about whether or not they had a shared future (that was a given), but about what kind of shared future they wanted to have.

Whether they like it or not, they have a shared future. What is true of them is also true of us as Christians. Christians have a shared hope. Nothing can change that. The question is what we will do with that shared hope. Will we allow ourselves to live in splendid isolation from one another, peeking over the fence at each other occasionally as either competitors or as enemies, or will we find one another, stand together, and serve together because we recognize that the ties that bind us are stronger than the spaces that divide us?

Having established the grounds of their unity in the opening verses of Ephesians 4 (there is one body and one Spirit), Paul reminds the Ephesian believers of their single calling and destiny:

> *There is one body and one Spirit, just as you were called to the one hope of your calling, one Lord, one faith, one baptism.*
>
> Ephesians 4:4–5

As we start to address this question, let's consider why Paul places this phrase here. There is a logical flow to the first two elements of the statement in Ephesians 4. One body with one Spirit that gives it life makes sense. Why, however, does he then go on to add the phrase, "just as you were called to the one hope of your calling"?

There are at least two good reasons why we find the calling of hope so strongly articulated here. Firstly, this calling sits at the very heart of the church's purpose. We are not called simply to exist for our own benefit. We are not some kind of heavenly social club on earth that awaits the imminent return of its groom and hides from the world in the meantime. We have a calling. We have a purpose. We have a reason for being. We are Christ's bride, and as such we point to Him. We exist so that God, through us, might bring more people into relationship with Himself. In the words of Martyn Lloyd-Jones:

The Church is not an end in and of itself; the Church is the body, the instrument which God is using through Christ and by the Holy Spirit to call out of mankind a new humanity, a new people for Himself, which He is finally going to perfect and cause to dwell in a renovated glorified world free from all sin.[71]

Secondly, the hope that sits within us is the hope of our own reunion with Christ and our own eternal life, which itself is grounded in the promised return of Jesus to the earth. This is deeply secured for us by the Holy Spirit Himself (Ephesians 1:13–14), so it is not a surprise that Paul places this great metaphor of hope at this point in his encouragement. As a pastor I have comforted many people with this promise of being with Christ. I have seen it dissolve fear and put a resolve of steel into someone who has become anxious about death.

A great many Christians today seem to dismiss the idea of heaven and the return of Christ. Perhaps it is because the church has been waiting for His return for so long. Perhaps it is because the idea of heaven itself has been debated and discussed for so long. Perhaps the reason is that more and more Christians seem to understand the idea of heaven as nothing other than another dimension of existence. I am sure all of these reasons, and others, could be given to explain the diminished presence of heaven and the second coming of Christ in so much modern preaching. Yet the fact remains that Jesus promised His disciples that He would return (for example, in John 14:3; Matthew 24:29–31); at His Ascension the angels clearly told the disciples that the same Jesus would return in the same way that they had seen Him depart (Acts

1:11); and the early church was comforted and strengthened by the hope of heaven and the promise of the return of Jesus Christ for His people (1 Thessalonians 4:13–18). This hope of Christ's return sat at the heart of the New Testament writers' encouragement to the early believers to live in holiness and faithfulness (see, for example, 1 Thessalonians 3:13; 1 Peter 1:14–16; 1 John 3:3). It was not just an idea or a theory for them; their hope was grounded in the promised appearance of Christ and the assurance that where He was, they would also be. Peter rooted his letter to the exiled believers in Asia Minor in this hope:

> *Blessed be the God and Father of our Lord Jesus Christ! By his great mercy he has given us a new birth into a living hope through the resurrection of Jesus Christ from the dead, and into an inheritance that is imperishable, undefiled, and unfading, kept in heaven for you, who are being protected by the power of God through faith for a salvation ready to be revealed in the last time.*
>
> 1 Peter 1:3–5

So on the one hand we have a sense of hope because we are called to point people toward God. We seek to lift the gaze of those around us from the world in which we live and the circumstances in which they find themselves and we point them toward a forgiving Father, a redeeming Son, and a powerful and present Spirit. We are a people of hope. On the other hand we have a sense of a shared hope as Christians because we know the end of the story. God wins. We know that one day the glory of the Lord will cover the earth as the waters cover the sea (Habakkuk 2:14). We have been told that one day every knee will bow and every tongue will confess that Jesus is Lord, to the glory of God the Father (Philippians 2:10). Christ will return. We will be with Him.

One day, sin, death, sorrow, and brokenness will be removed forever and there will be no more tears (Revelation 21:1–4). There is a simple phrase that has been attributed to many different people yet no one seems to really know where it comes from. The phrase is used by one of J. K. Rowling's characters in the *Harry Potter* series. It is heard in the film *The Best Exotic Marigold Hotel*, and it was used in the mid 1960s by John Lennon. It is, "It will all be okay in the end, and if it is not okay, then it is not the end." In a very simplified way, that idea sits at the heart of Christian hope for the future. The world may be a painful place, our lives may be hard, and we may well face persecution, ridicule, and ostracism, but we believe that God will put all things right in the end. We hold on to this conviction. We don't give up. We don't allow the pain of the present world to eclipse the hope of what God has already achieved in Christ and will ultimately demonstrate to the world.

These two realities are undoubtedly true. They have power to shape the way we view our current circumstances and they have the potential to lift others out of despair. That having been said, are these the only two ideas that shape our hope, and how does the idea of "one hope", as articulated here by Paul, unite us? In order to explore the one hope that we have been called to, let's explore the next few phrases in Paul's great declaration.

The faith we hold is rooted in the Christ we worship. In Him, we see the purposes of God come to fruition. We must be careful to remain true to the reality that Jesus Himself is the good news. In Him the purposes of God for Israel have been fulfilled and a life of bondage, fear, and brokenness has been overcome. To borrow a phrase from Scot McKnight, we must be careful not to turn the Christian faith into nothing more than "a sin management system" that secures our forgiveness and promises us a place in heaven when we die.[72] The Christian faith includes this marvellous and transforming hope, but it is much more than that.

One Lord, one faith, one baptism

United under one Lord

Paul, I think, defines his understanding of this shared hope himself when he uses these three phrases. In essence, he reminds the Ephesian believers that their unity is rooted in what has been done for them and not in what they can do for God. They are united by their common allegiance to Christ. Their social background is of little consequence. Their economic status is an irrelevance. Their position in society might be helpful for them, but it is not their defining characteristic. What unites them is what Christ has done for them. His life gives them life. His death rescues them from death. His atoning sacrifice has dealt with their sin. His resurrection assures them of resurrection. His promised return assures them that the end of the story is indeed one in which God wins.

We capture this focus on Jesus for the early church again and again in the New Testament, but nowhere more clearly than in Paul's letter to the Colossians. It is likely that the letter to the Colossians and the letter to the Ephesians are closely linked. Some even suggest that one is a variation of the other. When Paul writes to the Colossians, he reminds them of the absolute centrality of Jesus and what He has done for them:

He is the image of the invisible God, the firstborn of all creation; for in him all things in heaven and on earth were created, things visible and invisible, whether thrones or dominions or rules or powers – all things have been created through him and for him. He himself is before all things, and in him all things hold together. He is the head of the body, the church; he is the beginning, the firstborn from the dead, so that he might come to have first place in everything. For in him all the fullness of God was pleased to dwell, and through him God was pleased to reconcile to himself all things, whether on earth or in heaven, by making peace through the blood of his cross.

And you who were once estranged and hostile in mind, doing evil deeds, he has now reconciled in his fleshly body through death, so as to present you holy and blameless and irreproachable before him.

Colossians 1:15–22

See to it that no one takes you captive through philosophy and empty deceit, according to human tradition, according to the elemental spirits of the universe, and not according to Christ. For in him, the whole fullness of deity dwells bodily, and you have come to fullness in him, who is the head of every ruler and authority.

Colossians 2:8–10

Paul could not be clearer with the Colossians. Their old identity is gone and they have been given a new identity in Christ. That new identity cannot be taken away from them, and it is the source of their hope and the source of their unity. It is because of what Christ has done for them that they are brothers and sisters and therefore part of a new united family (Colossians 1:2); it is because of Christ that they share a relationship both with Paul and, more importantly, with God the Father (Colossians 1:1–2); it is their faith in Christ that has united them with the wider church (Colossians 1:4); it is what Christ has done that has transferred them from darkness to light (Colossians 1:13–14); Christ is the source of their new identity and hope (Colossians 2:2–3); Christ's death and resurrection has brought them from death to life and overcome sin and evil for them (Colossians 2:11–15); Christ alone now shapes the decisions they make, the priorities they set, and the lifestyles they choose (Colossians 3). Paul could not make it any clearer. This new community has been formed around the Lordship of Jesus Christ. They are His people. In the words of John Stott:

> For the Lord Jesus Christ is the one object of the faith, hope and baptism of all Christian people. It is Jesus Christ in whom we have believed, Jesus Christ into whom we have been baptised, and Jesus Christ for whose coming we wait with expectant hope.[73]

This sense of a new identity and a new purpose that flows from the Lordship of Jesus is seen throughout Paul's writings in the New Testament. It is this conviction that enables Paul to describe his own past as irrelevant when he writes to the Philippians. It is the same sense of the centrality of the Lord Jesus that gives Paul the boldness to challenge the cliques and the leadership cults that have developed in Corinth. When he writes to the Romans, he reminds them that Jesus is Lord, and therefore, by default, Caesar is not. The Lordship of Jesus demolishes old cultural and religious boundaries between the Jewish and the Gentile believers in Ephesus; it unites the slave owner with the slave as brothers in Paul's letter to Philemon; it removes the gender hierarchy and separation in Galatia; it obliterates the dividing lines between Cornelius and the Apostle Peter; and ultimately it is the supremacy and the majesty of the Lord Jesus Christ that will be acknowledged when every knee bows before Him (Philippians 2:10; Romans 14:11; Revelation 5).

United in the one faith

The New Testament knows nothing of the idea of entering into a negotiation of terms with the Lord Jesus Christ. In the book of Acts, every major sermon that is preached announces the Lordship of Jesus.[74] Indeed, the common theme of the Lordship of Christ through His life, death, resurrection, ascension, giving of the Spirit, and promised return, and its claim upon those who confess His Lordship now sit at the heart of what it means to be a disciple of Jesus. The Lordship of Christ and His claims upon His people are vital if we are to be united as disciples as opposed to consumers.

Consumers can pick and choose their product and develop an understanding of the Lordship of Jesus that suits their needs, affirms their principles, and is compatible with their preference. Disciples, on the other hand, have to take the rough with the smooth because they have abandoned their lives to the One whom they call Lord. Consumers can move from one shop to another if they become dissatisfied with what is on offer; they simply find a church that they enjoy more and leave the old one behind. Disciples, on the other hand, have come to understand that because Jesus is Lord every Christian is a brother or a sister and they are inextricably bound to all those who are part of the household of faith. Consumers can limit Christ's Lordship, curtail his commandments, and reshape his priorities. Disciples must lose their life to find His, they must pick up a cross to follow Him, and they must abandon their agendas for His.

The unifying power of the Lordship of Christ is that all Christians are called to surrender our lives to the life of Christ and to live in His power (the Spirit's power) and for His purposes (that the glory of the Lord might cover the earth as the waters cover the sea). This call to discipleship and to followership pulls us all from a primary affiliation or loyalty to a tradition, a denomination, or a movement and into a primary affiliation to the Lord Jesus Christ; or, to put it another way, to King Jesus. Our primary loyalty to Christ not only frees us from our social, gender, economic, and political affiliations of the past, it also frees us from giving an unhealthy priority to denominational distinctiveness that gets in the way of working with other brothers and sisters in the faith. Our denominational distinctiveness is not wrong. Much of it can actually provide variety, diversity, depth, and colour to the wider body of Christ. It is only when it becomes more important than our allegiance to the Lord Jesus that it becomes a negative influences in our lives.

Philippians 2 is probably one of the most famous sections of the New Testament among Christians. In it, Paul points to the example of the Lord Jesus Christ. He reminds the Philippians of Christ's great sacrifice for their sins, of His voluntary and temporary humiliation, and of His ultimate glorification. However, it is the reason for his use of the example of Jesus that is so challenging. Paul points to the example and the Lordship of Jesus in order to persuade the Philippian Christians to love one another and to set aside their own selfish agendas:

> *If then there is any encouragement in Christ, any consolation from love, any sharing in the Spirit, any compassion and sympathy, make my joy complete: be of the same mind, having the same love, being in full accord and of one mind. Do nothing from selfish ambition or conceit, but in humility regard others as better than yourselves. Let each of you look not to your own interests, but to the interests of others. Let the same mind be in you that was in Christ Jesus,*
> > *who, though he was in the form of God,*
> > *did not regard equality with God*
> > *as something to be exploited,*
> > *but emptied himself,*
> > *taking the form of a slave,*
> > *being born in human likeness.*
> > *And being found in human form,*
> > *he humbled himself*
> > *and became obedient to the point of death –*
> > *even death on a cross.*
> > *Therefore God also highly exalted him*
> > *and gave him the name*
> > *that is above every name,*
> > *so that at the name of Jesus*
> > *every knee should bend,*
> > *in heaven and on earth and under the earth,*
> > *and every tongue should confess*
> > *that Jesus Christ is Lord,*
> > *to the glory of God the Father.*
>
> Philippians 2:1–11

We are not free to construct a different faith. The faith that unites us is the faith that has been handed down to us. Some might call it the apostolic faith. Others might prefer to use the language of a faith that is consistent with the biblical narrative. Whatever language we use, we are not free to alter a gospel that has been handed to us with the strongest possible warnings not to alter it. Paul writes to both the Corinthians and the Galatians:

> *Now I should remind you, brothers and sisters, of the good news that I proclaimed to you, which you in turn received, in which also you stand, through which also you are being saved, if you hold firmly to the message that I proclaimed to you – unless you have come to believe in vain.*
>
> *For I handed on to you as of first importance what I in turn had received: that Christ died for our sins in accordance with the scriptures, and that he was buried, and that he was raised on the third day in accordance with the scriptures.*
>
> 1 Corinthians 15:1–4

> *I am astonished that you are so quickly deserting the one who called you in the grace of Christ and are turning to a different gospel – not that there is another gospel, but there are some who are confusing you and want to pervert the gospel of Christ. But even if we or an angel from heaven should proclaim to you a gospel contrary to what we proclaimed to you, let that one be accursed! As we have said before, so now I repeat, if anyone proclaims to you a gospel contrary to what you received, let that one be accursed!*
>
> Galatians 1:6–9

We are united under His reign and His rule. We are tied together as His subjects and citizens of His kingdom. He is the head and we are the body. He is our commander-in-chief, our captain, and our ruler. He is our role model and our source. We look to Him for instruction and for protection. We seek to do His will. These commitments to the Lordship of Christ are what unite His people around the world. Or at least they should be.

United through one baptism

The third component of the one hope that Paul is describing here is the unity that is brought about through baptism. Earlier in the book I explored the question of Holy Communion and the controversies it creates for many believers. I said I would address the issue of baptism later. I turn my attention to it for a moment now. For some, baptism in water is a covenantal act that can be performed on a child because of the promises of God spoken over or into the child's life through believing parents. They believe that it will be followed by a personal confession at a later date and that through that confession the act of baptism itself is either validated or becomes effective. For others, like me, baptism is a command to those who have surrendered to Christ. It is a declaration by a believer that they have entered a relationship with Christ and they want to be publicly identified with His death and with His resurrection. In both cases, baptism is part of the process of conversion and initiation into God's family. For a small number of Christians, baptism is no longer required.

How do I address the subject of baptism? If I speak of it out of my own convictions will I alienate those who believe it is right to have their children baptized? Is it an external expression of an internal conviction or is it an act of covenant? Do I upset those who believe that baptism carries some level of regenerative power by speaking of it as symbolic? What do I do about those Christian traditions that do not believe in any sacraments? What do I do about those Christian traditions that believe in more than two sacraments? It is a thorny and a controversial subject.

It is clear to me that the issue has to be addressed respectfully. I believe it is appropriate for a church with a tradition such as my own to maintain a strong commitment to baptism by immersion for believers while at the same time respecting the views of those who are part of a church which approaches the issue from a more covenantal position. I would always strongly encourage those seeking to come into partnership at the church I lead to be baptized by immersion as believers unless they have a strong conviction that their infant baptism, coupled with their confirmation, constitutes the same declaration of faith and entry point into the body of Christ. If the latter position were to be held strongly, then I would still welcome them into partnership in the church family and celebrate our common faith. I would find it difficult to welcome into membership those who have not been baptized and refuse to go through the rite. My reasoning is simple, I think. Paul clearly identifies baptism, in whatever form we believe it should take, to be both a distinguishing mark of the Christian and a unifying act for the believer. Through baptism we are each identified with the death and the resurrection of Jesus, but we are also each identified with one another in the body of Christ.

When someone is baptized, they are not simply being baptized into a denomination or a local church. The event of baptism may take place there, but the act of baptism is an entry point into the worldwide family of God. It is not a parochial affair; it is a universal affair. A baptism is an entry point into the great heritage of the church not only across the world in which we now live, but also across the church through the ages. By being baptized, we are taking our place alongside all those who have ever trusted Christ and all those who ever will. This act unites us to the family of God permanently and irrevocably. It declares to the world that we are Christ's and that we are sons and daughters of God.

In the early church, when someone was baptized, it often meant being cut off from their family. By declaring their allegiance to Jesus in such a way, they were declaring themselves to be part of a new family, the church. This was particularly true for Jewish believers. To become a follower of Jesus and to declare it through baptism was to turn their back on everything else. This is still the case in many parts of the world today. Many followers of Jesus from a Muslim background risk death for declaring their faith in Christ. I was present in Siberia a number of years ago when a pastor told a young woman who wanted to be baptized that if she decided to proceed she would almost certainly lose her job, her family, her home, and any chance of marrying (the latter because the ratio of female to male Christians was something like twenty to one). I was deeply moved as I heard her say that she still wanted to go ahead because she was now part of Christ's family and her place in it was far more important to her than anything else. Just under two years ago I was present as Muslims were baptized. A few months later I heard that one of them had been killed because of his allegiance to Christ.

These three great declarations of Paul are important for us as we think about Christian unity. A shared allegiance to the Lordship of Christ and His purposes brings with it a sense of common endeavour and shared commitment. A shared commitment to the apostolic faith roots us in the creeds and commitments that have held the church together for 2,000 years. A shared commitment to the life, death, and resurrection of Jesus and to taking a public and unapologetic stand for Christ unites us to the family of God around the world.

These three great realities bind us to God, but they also bind us to one another. They bind us to the purposes of God, the person of Christ, and the people of God. They are like deliberate stakes in the ground that announce to the world that we are not ashamed of following Jesus, we are not ashamed of what He teaches, and we are not ashamed of His family on the earth.

A shared hope

So the hope that we share is grounded in the Lordship of Christ, the apostolic faith we have received, and the witness and work of the worldwide church of Jesus. This is not simply a hope for a better future, although it is most definitely that. It is a hope – perhaps a better term might be a settled and convinced belief – that the power of the gospel and the Lordship of Christ still transforms lives and is still the only thing that can utterly turn a person's or a community's life around. It is a hope that shapes the choices we make today based on the convictions of what the future will look like. It is a hope that will see us willing to put ourselves in danger for the sake of brothers and sisters around the world who face danger every day simply because they are Christians.

This shared hope is a hope that affects the way we view ourselves, our world, and our place in it. It shapes how we speak of the world and its future. It shapes what we say about life after death. It shapes how we engage with politics, with culture, with business, and with the media. It shapes how we view work. It shapes our understanding of the environment and how we steward it. It shapes our views of other churches. This hope shapes everything. It reminds us that "we are but shadows of our future selves" and that the best is yet to be.[75] Our shared hope reaches back into our present from the future and changes the way we view ourselves and our purpose in the world. It is so certain that Paul could speak of our futures as already secured by using the past tense in his letter to the Romans:

> We know that all things work together for good for those who love God, who are called according to his purpose. For those whom he foreknew he also predestined to be conformed to the image of his Son, in order that he might be the firstborn within a large family. And those whom he predestined he also called; and those whom he called he also justified; and those whom he justified he also glorified.
>
> Romans 8:28–30

His convictions about the certainty of Christian hope meant that he was utterly convinced that our destinies were secured in Christ and that nothing could separate us from God's love, and therefore from God's purposes:

> What then are we to say about these things? If God is for us, who is against us? He who did not withhold his own

Son, but gave him up for all of us, will he not with him also give us everything else? Who will bring any charge against God's elect? It is God who justifies. Who is to condemn? It is Christ Jesus, who died, yes, who was raised, who is at the right hand of God, who indeed intercedes for us. Who will separate us from the love of Christ? Will hardship, or distress, or persecution, or famine, or nakedness, or peril, or sword? As it is written,

> *"For your sake we are being killed all day long;*
> *we are accounted as sheep to be slaughtered."*

No, in all these things we are more than conquerors through him who loved us. For I am convinced that neither death, nor life, nor angels, nor rulers, nor things present, nor things to come, nor powers, nor height, nor depth, nor anything else in all creation, will be able to separate us from the love of God in Christ Jesus our Lord.

Romans 8:31–39

Jurgen Moltmann, a German theologian and a former German prisoner of war, writes powerfully of hope in his seminal work, *Theology of Hope:*

The Christian Church has not to serve mankind in order that this world might remain what it is, or may be preserved in the state in which it is, but in order that it may transform itself and become what it is promised to be.[76]

He argues that the church is united by the power of God's purposes for the world being worked out in us and through us. He suggests that this shared mission should sit front and centre in our thinking, our relationships, and our behaviour:

> *Those who hope in Christ can no longer put up with reality as it is, but begin to suffer under it, to contradict it. Peace with God means conflict with the world, for the goad of a promised future stabs inexorably into the flesh of every unfulfilling present... This hope makes the Christian Church a constant disturbance in human society seeking as the latter does to stabilize itself into a "continuing city". It makes the Church the source of continual new impulses towards the realisation of righteousness, freedom and humanity here in the light of the promised future that is to come.*[77]

The power of a shared hope

I've been deeply moved in recent months as I have heard of different ways in which this sense of one hope has been impacting the church across the UK. When we grasp the potential of the gospel to impact our society through us, we find ourselves doing things that we never thought possible. Here are some examples.

Thy Kingdom Come

Between Ascension Day (25 May) and Pentecost (4 June) in 2017, hundreds of thousands of Christians around the UK will be uniting in a prayer and mission initiative called "Thy Kingdom Come". In 2016 the Archbishops of Canterbury and York invited parishes across England to join a great wave of prayer between Ascension and Pentecost. The response was overwhelming. Hundreds of thousands joined the wave of prayer in churches of many traditions and denominations around England and around the world. What began as an invitation in England started to look like the beginning of a global wave of prayer for people to know Jesus Christ.

For 2017 the vision is even bigger. The Presidents of Churches Together in England have joined with the Archbishops of Canterbury and York to make the call to churches of all denominations in England; Archbishop Justin Welby has sent out the call to every part of the worldwide Anglican Communion, and the World Methodist Council to Methodist Churches worldwide. The aims of the movement are simple: firstly, to join in prayer with the whole family of God the Father; secondly, to pray for the empowering of God's Holy Spirit; and thirdly, to pray that those involved will be effective witnesses to God the Son, the Lord Jesus Christ.[78]

One People Commission

The One People Commission is a body of the Evangelical Alliance in the United Kingdom (itself a unity movement for evangelicals) made up of key national church leaders who are committed to celebrating ethnicity while promoting unity within the UK evangelical church. The Commission is committed to finding new ways to celebrate the life of the Spirit across churches of different ethnicities. Bishop Eric Brown, one of the leaders in the Commission, has said:

> One of the greatest initiatives in recent years in Christendom in this country is the formation of the One People Commission, instigated by the Evangelical Alliance... for we believe that

we can spread the gospel of our Lord Jesus Christ better and more effectively when we do it together.[79]

Care for the Family

The power of a shared hope does not only impact congregational life and the ways in which denominations relate to one another; it also impacts families. This utter conviction that the gospel and the hope it brings has the power to transform lives is what led Rob Parsons to establish the charity Care for the Family. It runs events in partnership with local churches all over the United Kingdom to support families in local communities and to help them address difficult issues in their lives. From its courses that help parents to deal with the issues of drugs and substance abuse to its support of marriages and of those who are dealing with bereavement, Care for the Family is allowing the power of hope to shape the way in which it serves the family. It is utterly committed to partnering with local churches and with Christians from across the denominations.[80]

The Lighthouse Group

For some years now I have been supportive of a charity that was originally called The Lighthouse Group but is now known as Transforming Lives for Good. Its vision is simple: to bring hope and a future through education for children and families. It does this by working with young people who have either been forced to leave education because of behavioural or social problems or who have dropped out because of a sense of hopelessness and helplessness. The charity is deeply committed to its Christian values. Chief executive Tim Morfin is passionate about seeing the power of hope transform young people's lives. It runs a series of programmes alongside local churches as well as independent programmes through learning centres, which are making a real difference in the lives of young people across the United Kingdom.[81]

Hope Together 2018

Hope 08 began as a unity movement for mission and evangelism in 2008. Ten years on, it is still going strong. In fact, it is stronger than ever. In 2018 it is planning a year of mission and is gathering stories to inspire and encourage churches to get involved. It is partnering with all the major denominations and ministries, building together toward the year of outreach in 2018. Together they aim to mobilize the whole church in villages, towns, and cities, so people of all ages and ethnicities can discover the life-changing love of Jesus for themselves. They believe that the time is ripe for men and women and boys and girls to come to a living faith in the Lord Jesus Christ.

One of the things it is doing is to establish Mission Academies to help young people prepare to reach their peers and their communities, and to share their faith in creative ways. It is working with prison ministries to launch Prison Hope 2017, a year of mission in every prison to bring hope to prisoners and to encourage churches to engage with prisons. It has plans for city-wide missions in three major UK cities.[82]

It feels like almost everywhere I turn, I am hearing news of the church pooling its resources, finding new ways of engaging with the community, and sharing the gospel of the Lord Jesus Christ.

When we allow the things that unite us to come to the centre of our thinking and planning, we are stronger. There are hundreds and hundreds of stories that I could share of communities across the United Kingdom that are being impacted by local churches who are discovering the power of their shared hope. From Alpha courses being run across denominations in a local area, such as is happening in my own community in South Buckinghamshire, to Foodbanks[83] and Street Pastor[84] initiatives, local churches are working together more than they have ever done. And where they are working together, they are seeing great fruit.

Beyond unity for the sake of unity

The reality is that when churches work together and share resources and ideas, something happens. When their unity is nothing more than an occasional meeting or is forced by a formal structure, it does not necessarily produce life. Unity endeavours are hardly new. Writing in 1979, John Stott commented:

> *During the last half-century and more a great deal has been said and written about the unity of the church. The modern pre-occupation with it may be traced back to the influential, "Appeal to all Christian People" which was issued by the 1920 Lambeth Conference of Anglican bishops under the chairmanship of Randall Davidson, Archbishop of Canterbury.*[85]

Whether it be the inauguration of the church of South India in 1947 or the birthing of the World Council of Churches in 1948, there have been various ecumenical endeavours that have sought to unite churches. Where many of them have floundered is when they have lost sight of the missional element of unity. When churches commit to working together and serving together, something powerful happens. When they limit themselves to unity for its own sake, they seem to struggle. That may also be because an approach to unity that aims for the lowest common denominator is always going to prove dissatisfying. Unity that is not based on truth will not work. That is not to say that unity movements must agree on every jot and tittle of their theology or their creed, but it is vital for a healthy relationship of unity between Christians that there is a clear and shared commitment to, for example, the great Creeds of the Church. Ecumenism often fails because it seeks to avoid the difficult questions or it makes them less important than they should perhaps be.

In 1832 Thomas Arnold put forward a scheme to reunite dissenting bodies to the Church of England by the simple principle of widening the National Church to include them. This proposal was met with disdain by all who had a different idea of what it meant to be "the" Church in England. The Lambeth Conference of 1884 laid out what has become known as the Lambeth Quadrilateral. This outlined four points which might have made such a coming together as Arnold suggested possible. They were the wholehearted acceptance of the Scriptures as the record of God's revelation of Himself to human beings and the ultimate authority in issues of faith and doctrine; the acceptance of the Nicene Creed as a sufficient statement of Christian faith and the Apostles' Creed as a baptismal confession; the acceptance of the sacraments of baptism and the Lord's Table; and a ministry that carried the witness of the Spirit and the approval of the church. Yet there remain clear and apparently permanent divisions between the Church of England and the other Churches in England. This is not necessarily a bad thing, and perhaps the idea of institutional unity should be abandoned altogether because of the myriad differences that exist between the Anglican Church and so many of us who are not part of it.

The "Appeal to all Christian People" to which John Stott refers is a fascinating insight into the issues around institutional and structural unity. It acknowledges the importance of unity across churches and the challenge of different structures, offices, and institutions within both episcopal churches and non-episcopal churches. It also acknowledges the heartbreak of division in the body of Christ. In Article III we read:

> *The causes of division lie deep in the past, and are by no means simple or wholly blameworthy. Yet none can doubt that self-will, ambition, lack of charity among Christians have been principal factors in the mingled process, and that these, together with blindness to the sin of disunion, are still mainly responsible for the breaches of Christendom. We acknowledge this condition of broken fellowship to be contrary to God's will, and we desire frankly to confess our share in the guilt of this crippling the Body of Christ and hindering the activity of the Spirit.*[86]

The letter sounds good so far. It appears to bear the hallmarks of a genuine desire to address the issue of disunity across the church with a self-confessed humility and contriteness of heart. It goes on to argue for a new and fresh outlook on partnership in Article IV before reciting the Lambeth Quadrilateral in Article VI. In Article VII, however, it sets out a claim that the episcopate is the best body to approve ministers and clergy, and while it acknowledges the fruitfulness of ministries beyond the episcopate, in Article VIII it invites them to become validated by the episcopal office so that the church can be united again in a new body! What starts out well ends up with the sense that to achieve this unity, the dissenting churches would have to become episcopal, which strikes at the very principle of being non-conformist! Not surprisingly, the attempt at a new unity floundered.

The example of the 1920 letter is given to demonstrate that organizational and structural unity will always run into trouble if the structure and organization itself is given too much importance. Unity based on structures is an almost impossible endeavour. Perhaps it should not be sought. Unity that ignores truth will bring even greater dissension and chaos. An ecumenism that makes Christ, His purpose, and His mission anything other than central is also doomed to failure.

Unity that is built on a shared hope in Christ, the shared Lordship of Christ, a shared commitment to the apostolic faith, and a shared sense of belonging to the body of Christ is quite another thing. It is a pathway to a new and revitalized witness in the world, it is an answer to the permanently justified question of cynics as to why there are so many different strands of Christianity anyway, and it is a pragmatic and powerful pooling of resources for the furtherance of the kingdom of God and the uplifting of the name of Jesus. You do not have to compromise on your core convictions to work in unity with other Christians.

One God and Father of all

Paul's great sevenfold declaration of the unity of believers explores the reality that Christians are bound together because there is one body, one Spirit, one hope, one Lord, one faith, and one baptism, and he ties them all together by reminding the believers in Ephesus that there is "one God and Father of all, who is above all and through all and in all" (Ephesians 4:6).

As he encourages them to keep the unity of the Spirit in the bond of peace, he firmly roots them in the reality of their shared identity. Paul's basis of unity is not structural or organizational; it is relational. He reminds the believers that they find their value, their meaning, their significance, and their purpose in the Father. Some early manuscripts of this passage insert have a slight variation. They read, "there is one God and Father of all, who is above all and through all and in you all."[87]

The overwhelming textual evidence omits this addition of "you" in the last phrase, but the inference of it is surely seen in Paul's wider letter and in his epistles in general. This is not an appeal to the universal Fatherhood of God to all people. It is a reminder that God has entered into a special fathering relationship with all who have entered into a relationship with Him through His Son, Jesus Christ. We hear echoes of it across the rest of Paul's letter:

> *Grace to you and peace from God our Father and the Lord Jesus Christ.*
>
> Ephesians 1:2

> *I pray that the God of our Lord Jesus Christ, the Father of glory, may give you a spirit of wisdom and revelation as you come to know him.*
>
> Ephesians 1:17

For through [Christ] both of us have access in one Spirit to the Father. So then you are no longer strangers and aliens, but you are citizens with the saints and also members of the household of God.

Ephesians 2:18–19

For this reason I bow my knees before the Father, from whom every family in heaven and on earth takes its name.

Ephesians 3:14–15

Paul acknowledges in Ephesians 3 that all fatherhood and all families find their identity and meaning in the Fatherhood of God, but he also strongly ties the notion of intimacy with the Father with trust and faith in Christ. Our fundamental unity flows from our fundamental adoption into the family of God. It does not matter what our denominational tag is. It is of no eternal consequence what our preferred style of worship, church government, or preaching is. The thing that matters above all other things is that we have each been brought into a living relationship with our Father through His Son, Jesus Christ. We are brothers and sisters because we are sons and daughters. That cannot be changed. The reality of what He has made us forces us to think about how we treat one another.

Having explored the reality of the gift of unity that has been given to us through Christ by examining the prayer of Jesus in John 17, and having unpacked the core elements of that unity by exploring Ephesians 4:4–7, I now want to turn our attention to the fact that God has already promised to bless unity among His people, and we turn to that principle by reflecting on Psalm 133.

Reflection

If we genuinely have a shared obedience to the Lordship of Jesus, a shared identity through baptism and being part of God's family, and a shared sense of hope for the future, then what does that mean for how you do mission and ministry together as local Christians? Could you think about shared training for leaders or the possibility of running an Alpha course together?

There are some issues that affect all churches, such as educational choices for young people, the way in which we engage with the environment, the issues facing the wider local community such as housing and healthcare, and the broader challenges of what it means to have answers to the questions of those who are not yet Christians about other faiths, suffering, the reliability of the Bible, or the historical reliability of Jesus. Think about a shared approach to these issues. Could your churches run a united apologetics conference? Perhaps you could have a combined missions conference and as part of that have a careers fair for those thinking about university or for those who are approaching retirement? Could you partner with a group like A Rocha to deliver an eco-church programme in your community? Maybe you could think about campaigning together for the area to become a Fairtrade community?

Why not think about some opportunities to do some mission together, such as a combined overseas mission trip or a joined-up approach to welcoming refugees? Lastly, think about some joint training in evangelism for the local churches. How could you strategically approach the issue of sharing the good news of Jesus with every family in your community over the next five years?

The Blessing of Unity

How very good and pleasant it is
when kindred live together in unity!
It is like the precious oil on the head,
running down upon the beard,
on the beard of Aaron,
running down over the collar of his robes.
It is like the dew of Hermon,
which falls on the mountains of Zion.
For there the Lord ordained his blessing,
life forevermore.

Psalm 133

God has promised to bless His people when they live together in unity. That on its own should be a sufficient incentive for us to love one another deeply and to keep a commitment to walking together in mutual respect and honour at the top of our priority lists. If the prayer of Jesus in John 17 roots unity in the intimate relationship between Jesus and His Father, and the exhortation of Paul in Ephesians 4 roots it in the reality of the whole invisible church being the body of Christ on earth, enlivened by His Spirit, held under His Lordship, committed to His life and mission because all Christians are children of the same Father, then Psalm 133 sets out for us the beautiful promise of anointing, fruitfulness, attractiveness, and life that flows into us as the church and then through us into the world because of God's stated commitment to bless His people when they live in harmony with one another.

I have seen this blessing so many times. When Christians in a family commit to standing together, something wonderful happens. When I was pastoring a church in the south of England I became involved in a number of families that were falling apart.[88] Stephanie became a Christian not long after I arrived at the church in Springbourne. She was a lively, caring, and kind woman but she had lost her sparkle. Not long after she became a Christian she asked if she could come and see me. She had come to faith after a long battle with God. Her first husband had left her for another woman and she had been left to raise two daughters on her own. She had done a brilliant job. The betrayal of her first husband, however, had left her hurt, and she found it difficult to trust another man. Eventually she did meet someone – Robert – and they married. They had two sons and their lives seemed to be going okay until Robert started to stay away from home, money started to disappear from their account, and tensions started to rise. Stephanie noticed a pattern that she had seen with her first husband and began to wonder if Robert was seeing someone else. Her worst fears were confirmed when she discovered that he was having an affair. In desperation, heartbroken, and needing help, she turned to God. She found acceptance, hope, and purpose in her newly discovered faith, but she did not know what to do.

I met Robert a couple of times and talked to him about his life and his choices. It was very clear that he was also very unhappy. His affair was not giving him the joy and the significance that he had thought it would. He could also see the joy that was beginning to blossom in Stephanie's life. He wanted what she had, but he did not know how to find it.

After a few months Stephanie decided to be baptized and she asked me if I would talk to Robert about what it meant and why it was important. I happily agreed to do so. I will never forget the day I sat in their living room and explained to him Stephanie's faith and her decision to be baptized. After a little while Robert slid off his chair and on to his knees in the living room. With tears pouring down his face he asked me to lead him to Christ. He turned to his wife and begged her forgiveness for what had happened. He became a Christian, and instantly the atmosphere changed in their home. Stephanie decided to delay her baptism so that she and Robert could be baptized together. They started praying together, reading the Bible together, and attending church together. They addressed the issues that had divided them and set new principles into their marriage. Their two sons, both still living at home, also became followers of Jesus. The unity that their shared faith brought to them utterly transformed their lives. Now, more than twenty years later, they are still serving God together. I witnessed, first hand, the power of the blessing of unity in this family's life.

Some years later, I was involved in helping a church in the west of England. Their congregation had split over the departure of a previous pastor and they were in disarray. Over a period of around eighteen months I visited the church regularly. I met with the elders and the wider leadership team and helped them to talk through their disagreements and their hurts. I gave every single member of the church the opportunity to meet with me privately to discuss their own disappointments, concerns, and questions. The process took months of work and thousands of miles of travelling backwards and forwards to them from my home at the time. As they began to address the issues that were in the way of their unity, however, the church began to change. The hurts were addressed and the barriers that had been built began to be dismantled. At the end of the process we held a special service of healing and communion. I was moved to tears as I watched men and women who had somehow lost their relationship with one another rediscover their unity and commit to it again. I felt the very same sense of the commanded blessing of the Lord that I had sensed as I had watched Stephanie and Robert discover their unity. It was beautiful. It was powerful. That church continues to thrive. They have moved on, in a new-found confidence in what God is doing in them and through them. They have a new leader and the church has a new name. The sense of God's presence with them, guiding them, and blessing them is palpable.

God blesses unity among His people because it is His desire for His people. It doesn't matter whether that unity is seen in families, in congregations, or in cross-denominational partnerships and friendships. The same principles apply in any situation where unity is evidenced, and we can see those principles in Psalm 133.

The context of Psalm 133

Who wrote it?

It is not clear who wrote Psalm 133. Some early manuscripts ascribe it to King David and others do not. It is for that reason that some versions of the Bible in English, such as the English Standard Version and the Authorized Version, describe it as "A Song of Ascents. Of David", or "A Song of degrees of David" respectively, while others, such as the New Revised Standard Version, describe it as simply "A Song of Ascents". There is not enough strong evidence to make a firm decision either way. Personally, I tilt toward it being a psalm of David. If it is one that King David wrote, then it is not clear when he wrote it.

> *Whether it marked the moment he had waited for, when at last all Israel had rallied to him, and God had now given him Jerusalem (2 Samuel 5:1–10) or whether it was an isolated meditation, we have no means of knowing. David's later life lent tragic emphasis to his words, but here there is no trace of irony or regret. He had not yet exchanged this peace for the sword which would "never depart" from his house (2 Samuel 12:10).*[89]

If he wrote it at the beginning of his reign, then perhaps he was encouraging Israel not to break apart. There were always tensions between the ten northern tribes of Israel and the two southern tribes, even during the reigns of Saul, David, and Solomon. Eventually, after just three monarchs over the whole nation, the northern and southern kingdoms divided. They disagreed over the way in which funds were being raised by the king, and they parted company. If he was writing it at the end of his reign, then perhaps he was longing for them to return to a place of unity and mutual love and respect. If David did write the psalm, we do not have any way of knowing whether he was describing what he saw or describing what he longed for. Either way, if the words flowed from David's pen, we have a description of the people of Israel walking side by side, and the blessing God pours out upon such harmony relatively early in the life of the nation.

A second suggestion is that the psalm was written during the time of Nehemiah.[90] This would place it at the end of the story of the Old Testament. Nehemiah ministered in the fifth century BC and led the people of Israel to rebuild the wall in Jerusalem. Toward the end of his book, we have a description of the worshipping life of the people:

> Now the leaders of the people lived in Jerusalem; and the rest of the people cast lots to bring one of ten to live in the holy city Jerusalem, while nine-tenths remained in the other towns. And the people blessed all those who willingly offered to live in Jerusalem.
>
> Nehemiah 11:1–2

This context was one in which Jerusalem's walls had been rebuilt, but the city itself needed to be restored. The choice to live there was a hard one, wrought with danger and uncertainty. If the psalm was written during this time, then the encouragement of seeing people united and working together after having gone through a period of apostasy and division would have been more than enough to encourage the writer to gather their thoughts in praise to God.

Either way, the message of the psalm is the same. The writer is articulating the beauty of unity and the power it brings. They use the evocative imagery of the moment that Aaron and the high priests were anointed (Psalm 133:2) and of the deep, heavy dew that rested on Mount Hermon, many miles away (Psalm 133:3), to remind their readers of the blessing and the impact that unity has.

A song of ascent and a festival theme

The psalm is almost universally described as a song of ascent. This means that it was one of a series of psalms (Psalms 120–134) that were used by the people of Israel in their collective worship as they made their way to Jerusalem for one of the great festivals of the Jewish faith. The psalm would therefore have been sung by the people together as they enjoyed the festival, and I can imagine the strong sense of togetherness, companionship, and mutual affection. The festivals were a moment of celebration, of coming together, of reaffirming the shared bonds of faith and hope that knit the people of Israel into one family. It would have felt like the opening songs in some of the great contemporary Christian festivals as people gather from all over the country to celebrate their common allegiance to God. It would be a mistake, however, to assume that the unity described in the psalm is therefore restricted to the festival. It might be true to think that the unity of Israel was most clearly seen in these ancient traditions of gathering and celebrating, but it would be wrong to say that this is the only place that such unity existed. In fact, if that were the case, then the unity that they enjoyed would only be skin deep. The words of the psalmist describe something much deeper and more meaningful than that.

Christian festivals are vital for the health of the church. Building on the tradition of the Jewish festival principle, they draw Christians out of their normal context and into a new environment. They are disruptive to the everyday pattern of life and they create a new and a fresh space into which God can speak new things. He can remind us of what really matters, that we are not as isolated and alone as we might have thought, and that He is working in wonderful ways across the whole church. This kind of disruptive gathering is good for us, and it can certainly strengthen unity – but it cannot create it. A unity that is only expressed in an annual pilgrimage to New Wine, Spring Harvest, New Word Alive, the Keswick Convention, or any one of a number of other such events will not change the world. It might make us feel a little better, but unless that unity is carried on, unless it is embedded into the very heart of how we think and how we act, it will achieve very little. It is wonderful to celebrate unity in a large gathered event, but it is not enough. For the large celebration to mean something, there have to be roots into the local context. We need one another all the time, not just once a year for a few days.

What the psalm actually says

The psalm is actually very clear in its meaning, but the implications need a bit of unpacking. Fundamentally, it can be summed up by seeing the first and last sections as bookends, with the two word pictures in the middle of the psalm being used as illustrations for the overarching meaning. God loves unity and promises to always bless it:

> How very good and pleasant it is
> when kindred live together in unity...
> For there the Lord ordained his blessing,
> life forevermore.
>
> Psalm 133:1, 3

The two images that the writer uses to illustrate the way in which unity works are both taken from the story of Israel themselves. The first is the image of the anointing of Aaron, the High Priest:

> *It is like the precious oil on the head,*
> *running down upon the beard,*
> *on the beard of Aaron,*
> *running down over the collar of his robes.*

> Psalm 133:2

The image is taken from the scene of Aaron's anointing in the book of Exodus:

> *You shall take the anointing-oil, and pour it on his head and anoint him.*

> Exodus 29:7

> *The Lord spoke to Moses: Take the finest spices: of liquid myrrh five hundred shekels, and of sweet-smelling cinnamon half as much, that is, two hundred and fifty, and two hundred and fifty of aromatic cane, and five hundred of cassia – measured by the sanctuary shekel – and a hin of olive oil; and you shall make of these a sacred anointing-oil blended as by the perfumer; it shall be a holy anointing-oil… you shall consecrate them, so that they may be most holy; whatever touches them shall become holy. You shall anoint Aaron and his sons, and consecrate them, in order that they may serve me.*

> Exodus 30:22–25, 29–30

The second image is that of the heavy dew that rested on the slopes of Mount Hermon each morning:

It is like the dew of Hermon,
which falls on the mountains of Zion.

Psalm 133:2

Good and pleasant unity

Visibly beautiful

God loves unity, and He has promised always to bless it. That unity has an impact on the world and is visible to it. The unity that is described here carries a commanded blessing from God, not just an optional one.

When we read the words of the psalm carefully, we discover just how much God loves unity. It is "very good" and it is "pleasant" (verse 1). The implications of these two descriptions are important. Unity is both beneficial and enjoyable. It is beneficial because it brings with it blessings, and it is enjoyable because it connects us into better relationships in God's family, more resources, and therefore a shared sense of responsibility and obligation, and it makes the life of serving God more fun.

The second half of verse 1 is interesting. Some commentators suggest that the psalmist is pointing to a very specific form of unity, namely the idea of an extended family sharing their home together (for example, as described in Deuteronomy 25:5). Others have suggested that it refers to the formal unity of a gathered worship context because this is where the psalm would have been used. These definitions are helpful, but they are too narrow. They are helpful because they remind us of the importance of unity across our whole lives. How can there be unity in the church if there is not unity in the home, for example? Too often when we try to explore Christian unity we jump to the life of the congregation or to how one denomination relates to another. These are good areas to explore, but the seedbed of unity is in the private life of the individual and the life of the family. We can have all the unity that we want in public, but if our lives are broken in private it will have little impact. What good would it have done Stephanie or Robert to be part of a unified church if they themselves were not united in heart and mind and spirit? The psalmist is calling us to a deeper and more pervasive unity than that of the public gathering or the worship space only. He is calling us to unity that rediscovers the joy of common purpose in the home, in the extended family, in our workplaces, and in our wider lives of faith. The flowers of public unity grow in the soil of our private lives; our attitudes to those who are closest to us shape our attitudes to those who are further away. This is not some kind of dichotomous picture of unity; it is a holistic one:

> We believe rather that any and every kind of unity that can be observed among brethren is here praised as being most commendable.[91]

Tangible

The implications of these verses are immense. This isn't simply describing external and formal unity; it is not referring only to familial unity; it is not setting out an invisible unity, because it can be seen in the same way as Aaron being anointed can be seen and in the same way as the dew of Hermon can be seen: it can be sensed and experienced. This is a genuine unity of heart and mind and purpose.

THE BLESSING OF UNITY

There are a number of implications of the two images that the psalmist uses that can help us to understand the nature of the unity that God brings. The image of Aaron being anointed was one that those watching would have been part of. They would have experienced the benefit of the anointing. They would have smelt the oil and seen its presence. What was happening to them would impact them. In addition, the words from Exodus 30 about the anointing and its implications clearly show that the anointing of Aaron brought blessing and consecration to the other people of God. The same is true of the dew on Hermon. It was visible to all. In an arid and barren context it had an impact. God's unity, exhibited through God's people, has an impact on the world around us.

When the people in the church that I was helping in the west of England began to get out of the way and let God's unity flow through them, the whole community saw it. They felt it. They experienced it. One of the key markers of genuine unity is that it goes beyond lip service and is used by God to make a tangible, measurable difference in the lives of others. Unity, like love, always looks like something.

Flowing from God

It is interesting to note the way the language of the psalm develops. In our English versions of the text there is something that we miss. In the New Revised Standard Version of the Bible we read these three descriptions of the unity pictures in relation to Aaron's beard and to the dew on Mount Hermon in verses 2a, 2b, and 3a respectively:

... running down *upon the beard...*

... running down *over the collar...*

...falls on *the mountains of Zion.*[92]

In the Hebrew, however, there is a repeated phrase in each of these three images, and it is "descending". This unity now works its way out from within us; it works its way down into us and then flows from us. In other words, the unity that the psalm is describing flows from heaven to us. The oil used in the anointing of Aaron is a symbol of the Spirit's anointing. The physical oil, with its scent, its abundance, and its downward flow, is a picture of the anointing of God flowing over Aaron and from him into the atmosphere around him. The oil, however, was an outward symbol of the anointing of God upon Aaron. The same principle applies to the dew on Hermon. It came from heaven. This is the same principle for the unity described in the psalm. It is not made by people. It flows from God. As we have seen in Jesus' prayer in John 17 and Paul's encouragement in Ephesians 4, unity is not something that we strive to obtain; it is a gift from God that we strive to maintain. The flow is not from us to God. The flow is from God to us:

> In short, true unity, like all good gifts, is from above; bestowed rather than contrived, a blessing far more than an achievement.[93]

God is on the move in Reading in Berkshire and the surrounding area.[94] He is drawing people into faith, transforming lives, and building His church. In 2016 He started to draw people to faith through the visit of an evangelist from the United States. Hundreds of people have begun a relationship with the Lord

Jesus Christ and the impact is spreading to various parts of the United Kingdom, including Liverpool, Southampton, and other parts of the country. This is not something that has been initiated and caused by people, however. More than twenty years ago the leaders of the churches in Reading committed to praying together every week and celebrating one another's ministries. God had given them unity and they simply began to acknowledge it and let Him work through them. The result is... beautiful. Lives are being transformed because God's people are living together in the unity that He has given to them. If it can happen there, then why can't it happen in all of our towns and our cities? What do we do that stops the unity that God has given us to create the blessing that He promises? How can we get out of the way and let God do what God does best – change lives and transform communities?

Drawing people in

The unity described here spreads. Contrary to the idea that it only affected one or two people, the unity that is portrayed in Psalm 133 is both current and invitational. It is current in the sense that it is already there. This is what the writer is describing. It is also alluring. Like a magnet draws iron filings to itself, so this unity draws other believers in. It flows over the whole of Aaron, affecting his head and his heart. It flows off him and touches other people. As he touches others so does the oil, and therefore the impact of the anointing. The psalmist seems to be praising unity where it exists and commending it as something that is attractive and should be sought.[95] The inference of the descriptions of this unity is that it flows from the leaders to the people. It proceeds from the centre of the community out into the heart of it.

Israel may have been a led community, but it was also a community of equals. All who were part of Israel were equal in God's sight (Deuteronomy 15:3, 12; 25:3). It did not matter whether they were slaves, prophets, priests, or kings; they were, together, God's people. The picture of unity in Psalm 133 is a picture of a whole people drawn into greater intimacy and greater cooperation at every level.

What would happen if the church in the United Kingdom were to recognize one another more fully and were to make a choice to get out of the way and let the gift of unity that God has given us flow through us? So often we let structures, organizational needs, and secondary differences divide us. Surely people are more attracted to a unified and loving community than they are to a divided and unloving one? I am part of an online group on Facebook that is a space for ministers to ask for advice and share concerns and prayer requests. If it did that, I would be thrilled. Instead, I have found it to be a very negative environment. Ministers berate their deacons, their fellow elders, their congregations. They complain about the denomination they are part of, criticize their policies, and point out the flaws of the other churches in their community. It is a toxic environment to be part of and I don't like it, but I won't leave it. Instead, I try to speak well into it. I try to affirm people in it, to point out the things that the denomination is doing well, and to commend faithful elders, deacons, and local church leaders. Slowly, the tone is changing. It only takes one person to be committed to be a unifying voice for something to be transformed. Maybe God wants you to be that voice?

Most leaders know what it feels like to take responsibility for leading a group of people in a ministry that has become weighed down with criticism, cynicism, and control. It takes times to lead something from death to life. The first year can be really hard. Cultures of division and mistrust need to be overcome. We need to give constant permission for new ideas, instead of allowing them to be snuffed out. Creativity needs to be released and not restrained. Ministries that are riddled with division shy away from trying something new. The introduction of something new needs to be welcomed instead of being met with a heavy presence in the room that whispers in our ears that it didn't work last time so it won't work this time. Unity can change ministries. I have seen it happen again and again.

Unity brings out the best in people. I have watched beautiful leaders blossom in an atmosphere of unity in many areas of ministry of which I have the privilege of being part. They deliberately and intentionally choose to adopt an attitude that encourages us to stand together, to step out together, deliberately taking risks together, and growing together. I have listened as they have affirmed one another, watched as they have prayed for one another. I have been blessed by their support and love for me. I have been moved as they have prayed for me and carried me in their hearts in some of the most difficult times of my life. We can change the culture of what we are part of. We can get out of the way and let the gift of unity flow in us and through us. We can experience the blessing that God places on unity – we just have to be willing to be vulnerable and take the first step. When we do, we become more attractive.

Ministers' groups can become communities of life, support, and grace. Cynical and divided groups and ministries can be turned around. Unity brings with it new life, new passion, and new possibilities. Dying ministries and dying churches, and even dying denominations, can turn a corner and start to grow again. How? When we get out of the way and when we learn to celebrate one another, stand together, and allow God to take the centre of what we are doing, something changes. When we allow God to be our shared focus and when we commit to do what He wants to do together, then He will bless us. Unity commands a blessing.

The ordained blessing of life forevermore

The psalmist ends Psalm 133 with the other bookend of his statement. He begins the psalm by describing a good and pleasant unity. He ends it by declaring that God commands, or ordains, a blessing of life forevermore on such unity. Wow! If there is no other reason to allow God's unity to flow through us, surely this is reason enough? Not only is unity both effective and more fun, it also carries the commanded blessing of the Lord. And that blessing is life forevermore. Only God can give such a beautiful gift. He lets His life flow through His people when His people are flowing in His life.

A unified church is a drainpipe of hope to a broken world. We are a megaphone through which the voice of God can be heard more clearly. We are an instrument that He plays for His glory. Commenting on the promise of life forevermore contained here, Phil Moore says:

> Jerusalem received little rain and struggled with the fact it had no river; but David says that when God's People unite together they become a human river which flows to heal the nations.[96]

This metaphor of God's life flowing through us appears again and again in the Bible (see, for example, Psalm 36:8; 46:4; Ezekiel 47:1–12; John 7:37–39; Revelation 22:1–2), and in every instance the source of the water, and therefore the source of the life, is God Himself. Christians who are disconnected from one another become disconnected from God, and when we are disconnected from God, we have nothing to give the world around us. We cannot change anyone. We cannot give life to anyone. We cannot heal broken hearts. Only God can do these things. He is the One with the power of life. We do not need to worry about being the source of these things to people, however, because God has already promised that He will bring life forevermore to others through us, if only we will allow Him to do His work of unity in us.

I often think that if we truly understood the power of unity we would radically change the way we lived as Christians. Once you have seen its power, you will dismantle the ghettos of your prejudice and find a way of connecting with other Christians.

I will be visiting Rwanda in December 2016. By the time you read this book, my trip will be completed. The church in Rwanda has been working for almost twenty years on protecting their unity. The country was torn apart by genocide and hatred in the 1990s, and the church has been working together across denominations and streams in order to be conduits of God's peace. No one denomination can have an impact on the nation of Rwanda. It takes the whole church, the whole time, to make a difference. God has designed it this way.

A friend of mine, Dr Ruth Valerio, is passionate about the environment. She is the director of church engagement for the Christian charity A Rocha. She recently launched a project called

Eco Church.[97] Eco Church is an award scheme for churches in England and Wales who want to demonstrate that the gospel is good news for God's earth. Ruth knows that one denomination cannot change the church's perspective on climate and the environment, so she is committed to working with all churches to tackle the issue. Denominational boundaries are irrelevant when it comes to the future of the planet. God will bless a joined-up approach to the issue much more than He will bless a separatist and isolationist one.

Weaving the Threads Together

The life forevermore that God promises in Psalm 133 sounds remarkably like the abundant life that Jesus promises in John 10:10. The river of God in Ezekiel 47 is the same river that is described in Revelation 22. The great climax of the people of God is rooted in the hope of God and His purposes in the world. His aim is a new humanity that transcends race, culture, gender, and economics. The people of God come from every nation and tribe and people and tongue (Revelation 7:9). The ultimate work of God in His people will see the boundaries we have set removed, the fences we have built torn down, and the suspicion we hold for one another dissolved by perfect understanding and love. He invites us to walk in the gift of His unity now and to enjoy the benefits of it, because eternity will be spent with all Christians, not just the ones we like.

We have explored the powerful prayer of Jesus in John 17 for unity and we have discovered that it is rooted in the relationship between the Father and the Son. We have learned that God answers the prayers of His Son with a yes and that Jesus has prayed that we will be one just as He and His Father are one. We have been reminded that unity is not something that we strive to achieve but instead it is something that we strive to maintain. Exploring Paul's words to the Ephesians in chapter 4 of that letter we have been reminded that we are part of one body, inhabited by one Spirit, under the Lordship of one Saviour, rooted in one faith, and brought into the church through one baptism. All Christians, we have discovered, are brothers and sisters because we share one Father.

Then we looked at the promised blessings of unity contained in Psalm 133. These theological and biblical underpinnings help us to determine what our unity is and what our unity is not. They help us to have the right priorities when it comes to celebrating one another.

Reflection

We are not to reach down to the lowest common denominator but instead we celebrate the highest common identity, in Christ, by the Spirit for the Father. Our unity is not for its own sake but instead is missional. We are committed to one another so that the world might know that the Father has sent the Son. Our unity must be grounded in truth, seasoned with grace, rooted in love, and maintained by the ongoing presence and power of the Holy Spirit. We are not talking about an ecumenism that is weak but instead an ecumenism that is strong, rooted in the Bible, committed to the gospel, and ready to work together. Our unity is not seeking to make all faiths of equal truthfulness and value because we believe in the Creeds. We are Christians. We do not want to put our denominations before our God but nor do we want to dismiss our denominational distinctiveness. We are to be committed to one another because we are committed to Christ. We have seen that unity is a vital issue for individuals, for families, and for communities, not just for denominations and congregations. Our commitment to unity could change our homes, our workplaces, and the areas where we live. What would need to happen in us for this to be a visible reality?

Why, then, is it so hard? What are the jagged edges of unity and how do we go about addressing them? What does it look like for the church to be united in mission and in the gospel? How do we address the issues that threaten to divide us, such as sexuality, the role of women, the place and function of the Bible, and so forth? How do we stand with our brothers and sisters across the world who are facing danger and death? Is there a way for the church to cross generational divides? How do local churches put aside their differences for the good of the communities they are part of? How do we respect the personhood of someone with whom we deeply disagree? Can our disagreement itself be handled in such a way that it becomes a gift to the wider world and points to the mercy and the grace of God?

Now that we are armed with a greater level of theological and biblical insight, the challenge lies in what the implications of this unity are. In this volume I have sought to set out the foundations of our unity. We must now turn our attention to the implications of the unity that God has given us. These implications are so profound and so demanding that they demand a second volume in which to be explored. Having laid the groundwork, we now turn our gaze to making the gift of unity into a tangible demonstration of the grace and mercy of God in Christ. That is the subject of *One for All: The Implications*.

Notes

Unity Matters

1. For an outline of the issues in the debate and its repercussions see Andrew Grills, "Forty Years On: An Evangelical Divide Revisited". Available at http://archive.churchsociety.org/churchman/documents/cman_120_3_grills.pdf (last visited 23 January 2017).
2. See J. Brencher, *Martyn Lloyd-Jones (1899–1981) and Twentieth Century Evangelicalism* (Carlisle: Paternoster, 2002), p. 90.
3. See Timothy Dudley-Smith, *John Stott: A Global Ministry* (Leicester: IVP, 2001), p. 68.

We're Family

4. Harper Lee, *To Kill a Mockingbird* (London: Arrow Books, 1960), chapter 23.
5. The root word from which we have the word "apologist" is *apologia* and means a defence, especially of one's opinions, position, or actions.
6. "See how these Christians love one another". Available at https://www.christianhistoryinstitute.org/magazine/article/see-how-these-christians-love/ (last visited 30 January 2017).
7. The word "catholic" here simply means universal.
8. *On the Unity of the Catholic Church* written by St Cyprian of Carthage for the Council of Carthage in AD 251. Available at https://www.christianhistoryinstitute.org/study/module/cyprian/#toc_item1 (last visited 23 January 2017).
9. The word *traditores* means "the ones who handed over the book".

God's Plea

10. Based on 1 Corinthians 1:10.
11. Based on Ephesians 4:11–13.
12. Based on Romans 12:4.
13. Based on Colossians 3:13–14.
14. Based on John 17:20–23.

15. Based on Psalm 133.
16. Based on 1 Peter 3:8.
17. Based on Ephesians 4:3.
18. Based on 1 John 4:12.
19. Based on Romans 12:16.
20. Based on Matthew 23:8.
21. Based on Ephesians 2:14.
22. Based on Philippians 2:1–11.
23. Based on Galatians 3:26–28.
24. Based on 1 Corinthians 12:12–13.
25. Based on Ephesians 4:16.
26. Based on Romans 6:5.
27. Based on 1 Corinthians 1:10.

Confessing Our Division

28. See http://www.cinnamonnetwork.co.uk/our-story/ (last visited 24 January 2017).
29. See http://www.gather.global/ (last visited 24 January 2017).
30. Malcolm Duncan, *Kingdom Come: The Local Church as a Catalyst for Social Change* (Oxford: Monarch Books, 2007), pp. 212–213.
31. Sean Oliver-Dee, *God's Unwelcome Recovery* (Oxford: Monarch Books, 2015), pp. 14ff.
32. Oliver-Dee, *God's Unwelcome Recovery*, p. 14.
33. Malcolm Duncan, *Building a Better World: Faith at Work for Change in Society* (London: Continuum, 2006), pp. 4–5.

Christ's Cry for His People – That We May Be One

34. W. Milligan and W. F. Moulton, *Commentary on the Gospel of John* (Edinburgh: T. & T. Clark, 1898), p. 188.
35. Tom Wright, *John for Everyone: Part 2, Chapters 11–21* (London, Society for Promoting Christian Knowledge, 2002), p. 92.
36. See, for example, Leon Morris, *The Gospel According to John* (London: Marshal, Morgan and Scott, 1972), p. 716.
37. See, for example, C. K. Barrett, *The Gospel According to St. John* (Philadelphia: The Westminster Press, 1978), p. 500.
38. Ian Paul's reflections on John 17 are very helpful for navigating what lies at the heart of Jesus' prayer in John 17. See http://www.

psephizo.com/biblical-studies/is-john-17-about-unity/ (last visited 24 January 2017).

39. J. C. Ryle, *Expository Thoughts on John Volume 3* (Edinburgh: Banner of Truth trust, 1987), p. 226.

40. D. A. Carson, *The Gospel According to John* (Nottingham: Apollos Press, 1991), p. 568.

41. A. W. Tozer, *The Pursuit of God* (Milton Keynes: Authentic Media, 2004), pp. 68-69.

42. See www.changingattitude.org.uk for more information (last visited 24 January 2017). Changing Attitude and the Lesbian and Gay Christian Movement (http://www.lgcm.org.uk/ – last visited 24 January 2017) have recently announced plans to merge.

43. See www.acceptingevangelicals.org for more information (last visited 24 January 2017).

44. See www.livingout.org for more information (last visited 24 January 2017).

45. See www.eauk.org for more information (last visited 24 January 2017).

46. See http://www.somethingtodeclare.org.uk/statement.html for more information (last visited 24 January 2017).

47. Morris, *The Gospel According to John* p. 734.

48. Barrett, *The Gospel According to St. John*, p. 512

49. William Barclay, *The Gospel of John Volume 2* (Edinburgh: The Saint Andrew Press, 1956), p. 254.

50. Barclay, *The Gospel of John Volume 2*, p. 255.

51. Wright, *John for Everyone*, p. 100.

52. See Barclay, *The Gospel of John Volume 2*, p. 256.

One Body – A Shared Family

53. D. Martyn Lloyd-Jones, *Christian Unity: An Exposition of Ephesians 4:1–16* (Edinburgh: The Banner of Truth Trust, 1980), p. 52.

54. Lloyd-Jones, *Christian Unity*, p. 56.

55. Lloyd-Jones, *Christian Unity*, p. 64.

One Spirit – A Shared Life

56. See Francis Foulkes, *Ephesians* (Leicester: Inter-Varsity Press, 1989), p. 120.

57. Ephesians 4:4.

58. 1 Corinthians 12:13.

59. John Stott, *The Message of Ephesians: God's New Society* (Leicester: Inter-Varsity Press, 1979), p. 150.

60. See Tom Kraeuter, *If Standing Together is so Great, Why Do We Keep Falling Apart? Real Answers to Walking in Unity* (Hillsboro, Missouri: Emerald Books, 1998), p. 38.

61. As quoted in Tim LaHaye, *Spirit-Controlled Temperament* (Eastbourne: Kingsway Publications, 1978), p. 16.

62. John Calvin (translated from the original Latin by the Rev William Pringle), *Commentaries on the Epistles of Paul to the Galatians and Ephesians* (Grand Rapids: Baker Book House, 1989), pp. 268ff.

63. Calvin, *Commentaries*, p. 268.

64. Geoffrey Wainwright, *Embracing Purpose: Essays on God, the World and the Church* (Peterborough: Epworth, 2007), p. 210.

65. Pete Greig, *Dirty Glory: Go Where Your Best Prayers Take You* (Colorado Springs: Navpress, 2016), pp. 282ff. The chapter entitled "Dirty Dancing" is a powerful call to unity which is only possible through humility.

66. "The cost and the joy of unity – reflections on the Primates' meeting in Canterbury", 21 January 2016. Available at http://www.archbishopofcanterbury.org/blog.php/26/the-cost-and-the-joy-of-unity-reflections-on-the-primates-meeting-in-canterbury (last visited 25 January 2017).

67. "Christian unity will grow step by step, says Pope Francis", *Catholic Herald*, 27 January 2014. Available at http://www.catholicherald.co.uk/news/2014/01/27/christian-unity-will-grow-step-by-step-says-pope-francis/ (last visited 25 January 2017).

68. There are various references to this quotation available on the internet, but I am yet to source the original quote itself. For example, see http://www.patheos.com/blogs/robertcrosby/2012/05/a-w-tozer-on-the-holy-spirit-todays-church/ (last visited 25 January 2017).

69. Gordon D. Fee, *God's Empowering Presence: The Holy Spirit in the Letters of Paul* (Peabody: Hendrickson Publishers Inc., 1994), pp. 901–902.

One Hope, One Lord, One Faith, One Baptism – A Shared Future

70. Its full title is "A Shared Future: Policy and Strategic Framework for Good Relations in Northern Ireland". Available at https://www.executiveoffice-ni.gov.uk/sites/default/files/publications/ofmdfm_dev/a-shared-future-policy-2005.pdf (last visited 25 January 2017).

71. Lloyd-Jones, *Christian Unity*, p. 83.

72. Scot McKnight, *The King Jesus Gospel: The Original Good News Revisited* (Grand Rapids: Zondervan, 2011). Chapter 2, (pp. 28–33), entitled "Gospel Culture of Salvation Culture?"; chapter 3 (pp. 34–44), entitled "From Story to Salvation"; and chapter 5 (pp. 63–77), entitled "How Did Salvation Overtake the Gospel?" are particularly enlightening. I am not sure that McKnight's exegesis of 1 Corinthians 15 in chapter 4 (pp. 45–62), under the heading "The Apostolic Gospel of Paul" sufficiently addresses the clarity with which Paul embeds the good news of Christ in Jesus' death, burial, and resurrection for our sins, which it seems are central in both Paul's understanding of the purpose of Jesus and in Jesus' understanding of His own ministry. Indeed, it feels like McKnight has to bend the straightforwardness of Paul's clear message in 1 Corinthians 15 to make it fit McKnight's overarching purpose. Perhaps that is the challenge of systematic theology, which has to blend the truth of Scripture, compared to biblical theology, which is content to exegete the text and allow apparent contradictions to create a healthy tension. That being said, McKnight is right to challenge a gospel which stops at the cross and does nothing to tell the story of the life and overarching purpose of Christ. We cannot access God's grace without the cross and the atoning sacrifice of Christ for us there, and we cannot understand what Christ has done for us without seeing the cross at the centre of His whole life and ministry. The good news rescues us from our sin and brokenness but it also gives our lives purpose, identity, and meaning within a world that is being transformed by God through His Son and His Spirit.

73. Stott, *The Message of Ephesians*, p. 150.

74. See Acts 2:14–40; 3:12–26; 4:5–12; 10:28–47; 11:4–18; 13:16–41; 14:15–17; 15:7–11; 17:22–34; 20:17–35; 22:1–21; 24:10–21; 26:2–23; 28:17–22.

75. The phrase, "we are but shadows of our future selves", is a chapter heading in a book on the power of hope and eschatology which was published for Spring Harvest 2008. I find the chapter title deeply evocative. It conjures up in me a longing to become what God has already promised me I am. See Stephen Holmes and Russell Rook (eds), *What Are We Waiting For?* (Milton Keynes: Paternoster, 2008), pp. 212–222. The book also has excellent chapters addressing issues such as ecology and environment by Ruth Valerio and the dangers of an over-realized eschatology or an extreme and literalist view of end times by Stephen Holmes.

76. Jurgen Moltmann (translated by James W. Leitch), *Theology of Hope* (London: SCM Press, 1967), p. 327.

77. Moltmann, *Theology of Hope*, pp. 22–23.

78. For more information see http://www.thykingdom.co.uk/ (last visited 26 January 2017).

79. For more information see http://www.eauk.org/church/one-people-commission/ (last visited 26 January 2017).

80. For more information see https://www.careforthefamily.org.uk/ events (last visited 26 January 2017).

81. For more information see http://www.tlg.org.uk/ (last visited 26 January 2017).

82. For more information see http://www.hopetogether.org.uk/ Groups/272232/Towards_2018.aspx (last visited 26 January 2017).

83. For more information see https://www.trusselltrust.org/ (last visited 26 January 2017).

84. For more information see http://www.streetpastors.org/ (last visited 26 January 2017).

85. Stott, *The Message of Ephesians*, p. 147.

86. Henry Bettenson and Chris Maunder (eds), *Documents of the Christian Church* (Oxford: Oxford University Press, 1999), pp. 412–413.

87. Stott, *The Message of Ephesians*, p. 150.

The Blessing of Unity

88. To protect their identities and honour their dignity, I have changed their names.

89. Derek Kidner, *Psalms 73–150* (Leicester: IVP, 1975), p. 452.

90. H. C. Leupold, *Exposition of Psalms* (Welwyn: Evangelical Press, 1977), pp. 917ff.
91. Leupold, *Exposition of Psalms*, p. 917
92. Emphasis mine.
93. Kidner, *Psalms 73–150*, p. 134.
94. For more information see http://www.ukrevival.org/2016/06/god-is-moving-in-reading/ (last visited 26 January 2017).
95. Leupold, *Exposition of Psalms*, p. 917.
96. Phil Moore, *Straight to the Heart of Psalms: 60 Bite-sized Insights* (Oxford: Monarch, 2013), p. 242.
97. For more information see http://ecochurch.arocha.org.uk/ (last visited 26 January 2017).